# FOREWORD

Liverpool Cathedral is arguably the finest British building of the 20th century. It occupies a special place in the hearts of the people of Merseyside, and seldom fails to evoke a sense of awe in those who visit it for the first time. It remains what it has been since even before the laying of its foundation stone: 'A safe place to do risky things in Christ's service'.

Its capacity to startle (by its sheer size, by its classical 'Gothic'-ness) those who have not encountered it before is well known. But as these Chronicles will amply demonstrate, it is also a building which retains the capacity to surprise those who think they know it well.

Roy Redman knows Liverpool Cathedral better than most people. He has produced a highly engaging and informative guide, full of factual nuggets arranged chronologically, some very familiar but others much more arcane. It is a book which will delight those who read it and which is sure to establish itself as a standard resource for many years to come. It is my great pleasure to commend it.

**The Revd Dr. Pete Wilcox**
Dean of Liverpool, August 2015

*The Revd Dr Pete Wilcox*

*Photo: © Gerry Simons*

# ACKNOWLEDGEMENTS

*My warm thanks to Dean Pete Wilcox for his support in the publishing of the book. My gratitude to Kevin Stott, the Cathedral retail manager, who has supported the publication of the book from the very beginning, when I first put forward the suggestion to publish such a work. My thanks to Gerry Simons of Taylor Simons Design for the graphic design and production of the book. My thanks to Canon Val Jackson, the Cathedral archivist, for patiently locating various documents, and in particular, identifying photographs not previously published. To Geoff Shipley my gratitude for always being willing to help with my requests to photograph inside and outside the Cathedral. To my great friend the Revd Colin Sands, my thanks, for reading the first draft of the manuscript with a critical eye. His comments and suggestions were always considered and constructive. To the Cathedral Company, and those family members with ancestors who worked in and on the Cathedral, my gratitude, for sharing with me your Cathedral memories.*

# ROY REDMAN

*Photo: © Gerry Simons*

*Roy, who is Head Guide at the Liverpool Cathedral, has been a worshipping member of the Anglican church since 1946 when he became a choir boy at St John and St James Parish Church, Bootle. This was followed, for many years, as an active church member of Christ Church, Bootle, serving in many roles, including in the early 1970s being a member of the Deanery Synod and the Diocesan Synod. Roy was a member of the first GUML (Group for Urban Ministry and Leadership) team commissioned by Bishop David Sheppard in 1989. He has been a worshipping member of the Cathedral for the past fifteen years and a Cathedral volunteer for over ten years. Roy is married to Valerie, a retired nursing sister. They have two daughters Claire and Rachael, who are both head teachers. Roy and Valerie have three grandchildren.*

*Roy is also co-author of Bootle Milestones and Bootle Sign Posts.*

# PREFACE

WELCOME TO CATHEDRAL CHRONICLES containing a veritable variety of interesting facts, figures, events and anecdotes that have occurred during the period from 1878, when the See of Liverpool was created, to the completion of the Cathedral building in 1978.

Many visitors to the Cathedral, whilst acknowledging the splendour of the building, wish to know why such a large Cathedral was built. The answer was given on June 17th 1901 and is recorded as follows; First, the Cathedral "would be a witness for God in the midst of this great city, Secondly, "the Cathedral was needed for diocesan and popular services. "Thirdly, the Cathedral "would express and deepen the spiritual longings and aspirations of many among them'. Lastly, 'it must be the building of all classes".

The common purpose which has united all who have given and worked for this Cathedral has been the worship and glory of God. Exemplified by the architect Sir Giles Gilbert Scott, who had with him, artists, engineers, craftsmen, glaziers, embroiderers, carpenters, joiners and masons, the men who worked the quarry, men and women known and unknown, skilled and unskilled, each making their special contribution in the stone, the metal, the wood, the glass and the fittings which adorn the Cathedral. Many of their names are recorded here but it is with thanksgiving we remember all who under the visionary and inspiring leadership of Bishop Chavasse and often in the face of many difficulties achieved the goal of building this wonderful Cathedral. Their memorial is captured in the *Laymen's* window "Remember with thanksgiving all those who by diversity of talents and unity of purpose built this Cathedral to God's glory."

The Cathedral, as 'the mother church', of the Diocese has played, and continues to do so, a major role in the life of the city. Times of joy and sadness, times of war, industrial and sectarian strife have been witnessed and so to reflect the background of the era in which the Cathedral was being built some diocesan, local and national events are recorded.

The result of my research has, I hope, created an interesting mine of information that will appeal to a wide range of readers, from the casual enquirer, to those with a real interest in the history of the Cathedral. Information that readers can dig into again and again. Whilst I have made every effort to be accurate with names and dates, in such a work omissions and errors may occur and apologies are expressed for any data that may be open to query. Additions and corrections from any source would be gratefully received for inclusion in any future revision.

*"The Cathedral will outlast the centuries and be a daily inspiration to the stream of people who pass by it."*
*Canon James Bezzant, Canon Residentiary and Chancellor from 1932 to 1952.*

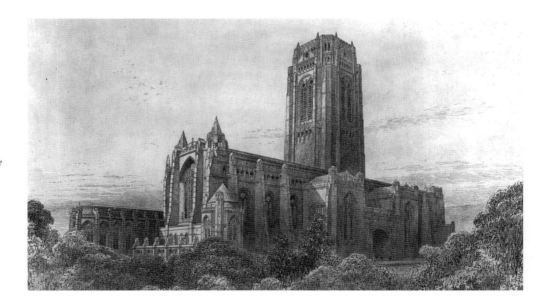

*We had to look for that power combined with beauty that makes a great and noble building. In the set of drawings by Mr. G. Gilbert Scott we find these qualities pre-eminently shown, we cannot but give it first place.*
Mr. George F. Bodley and Mr. R Norman Shaw

*Masons at work on Liverpool cathedral.*

# 1878

*On August 16th the Home Secretary Lord Richard A. Cross (1823/1914), who was MP for South West Lancashire, introduced and succeeded in passing the Act of Parliament (Bishoprics Act) which created the See of Liverpool.*

*Bishop Ryle*

*On April 16th 1880 The Revd John Charles Ryle, Vicar of Stradbroke, Suffolk and Dean-designate of Salisbury was appointed by Lord Beaconsfield (Benjamin Disraeli) as the first Bishop of Liverpool.*

## 1878

On August 16th the Home Secretary Lord Richard A. Cross (1823/1914), who was MP for South West Lancashire, introduced and succeeded in passing the Act of Parliament (Bishoprics Act) which created the See of Liverpool. The area of the See was bounded by Southport, Wigan, Newton-Le-Willows, Warrington, St.Helens, Wigan and Liverpool, covering an area of about 300 square miles.

Sir James A. Picton (1805/1889), the Liverpool born historian and architect, raised in the public press the question of the site for a Cathedral for the contemplated Diocese.

## 1880

The Liverpool Diocese was founded on March 24th separating it from Chester. St Peter's Church in Church Street, which was consecrated in 1704, became the Pro-Cathedral.

The Diocese was divided into two archdeaconries and nine rural deaneries. The archdeaconry of Liverpool was first created on August 10th 1847 in the Diocese of Chester.

Canon John H. Jones, Vicar of Christ Church, Waterloo, remained the Archdeacon of Liverpool, a position he had held from 1855. Canon J. W. Bardsley, Vicar of St. Saviour's Church, Falkner Square, was installed as the first Archdeacon of Warrington in the newly established archdeaconry of Warrington and twenty four honorary Canons were appointed.

On April 16th The Revd John Charles Ryle, Vicar of Stradbroke, Suffolk and Dean-designate of Salisbury was appointed by Lord Beaconsfield (Benjamin Disraeli) as the first Bishop of Liverpool. Bishop Ryle, accompanied by his wife Henrietta and son Herbert, made his first official visit to Liverpool on April 22nd.

On April 21st it was announced that Liverpool would be granted 'City status' on May 11th.

The Revd Ryle was consecrated Bishop of Liverpool at York Minster on St Barnabas Day, June 11th by the Archbishop of York, the Most Revd William Thomson (1819/1890).

Church bells rang throughout the city when Bishop Ryle was enthroned the first Bishop of Liverpool in St Peter's the Pro-Cathedral on July 1st. The sermon was preached by the Dean of Chester the Very Revd John Howson (1816/1885).

On September 19th Bishop Ryle ordained the Revd William James Adams (1839/1903), the first ordination of his episcopacy. The Revd Adams, who was Chaplain to the British Indian Army, was awarded the Victoria Cross during the Second Afghan War. He was the first clergyman to receive the award.

On November 9th Giles Gilbert Scott was born at 26 Church Row, Hampstead, London, the third son of the architect George Gilbert Scott jnr. (1839/1897) and Ellen Gilbert Scott (1854/1953).

To mark the creation of the Diocese Mrs. Jane Lawrence, a member of the Earle family, presented a silver gilt service.

Sir William Bower Forwood (1840/1928), who played a major part in the founding of the Cathedral, was elected Mayor of Liverpool.

## 1881

On November 16th and 17th in St George's Hall, Bishop Ryle presided at the first Liverpool Diocesan Conference. The conference was open to the clergy of the Diocese and two elected lay representatives from the parishes. On Bishop Ryle's initiative a commission conducted a systematic inquiry into the needs of the Diocese. As a result parochial boundaries were redrawn, and churches removed from the less populous areas of the city to the suburbs.

Bishop Ryle took up residence at The Bishop's Palace, 19 Abercromby Square, Liverpool.

## 1882

On June 24th The Walton Vicarage Bill, promoted by the trustees of the Liverpool Bishopric Fund, received the Royal Assent. As a result the trustees were able to purchase the advowson for £28,000 and raise the Bishop's stipend to the maximum, fixed by Act of Parliament, of £4,200.

# 1889

*Bishop Ryle informed the Prime Minister Lord Salisbury (1830/1903) of the importance of appointing an Archdeacon of Liverpool with whom, 'I can cordially co-operate'.*

*New Church House, situated on the corner of Lord Street and North John Street.*

On Trinity Sunday Bishop Ryle arranged a diocesan census. The census recorded 165,000 people attending an Anglican service.

The Arms of the Diocese of Liverpool were granted by the College of Arms. The Diocesan Arms, on a lozenge, are incised into the central bay of the Choir. The arms contain the Mitre, the liturgical head-dress of a bishop, the Eagle allotted to St John (John was the Christian name of the first bishop), the inkhorn in the eagle's claw refers to the recording of St John the Evangelist's vision on the Isle of Patmos, the ancient ship the Lymphad, representative of the maritime origin of the City of Liverpool, and the Bible is given special prominence at the request of Bishop Ryle, to show that the basis of all Christian teaching in the Diocese was to be scriptural.

## 1883

The Rt Revd Edward Benson (1829/1896) was appointed Archbishop of Canterbury. In 1880 he devised the Festival of 9 Lessons and Carols. The service was used for the first time at Truro Cathedral.

## 1884

Archbishop Thomson of York visited Liverpool.

On October 17th Bishop Ryle consecrated St Lawrence's Church, Barlow Lane, Kirkdale. During his twenty year episcopate twenty four new churches were built in the Diocese. The last church to be consecrated by Bishop Ryle was Emmanuel, Southport on April 16th 1898.

## 1885

By Act of Parliament a Cathedral Building Committee was established. The committee after considering twenty three sites authorised the erection of a Cathedral on the site of St. John's Church (demolished in 1898) situated adjacent to St George's Hall.

## 1886

On May 11th Queen Victoria visited Liverpool to open the International Exhibition of Navigation, Commerce and Industry. In the presence of Royal and Civil dignitaries, Archbishop Thomson of York was accompanied by Bishop Ryle who led a short service. During the Queen's visit the Mayor of Liverpool, David Radcliffe, was knighted. His son Frederick was to play a major role in the founding of the Cathedral.

As a result of a competition to design a Cathedral, the architect Sir William Emerson's (1843/1924) submission for a domed Gothic Cathedral, sited immediately below St George's Hall, was approved by Mr. Ewan Christian (1814/1895) architect to the

Ecclesiastical Commissioners. Due to lack of support the scheme to build a Cathedral was aborted.

Canon John H. Jones resigned as Archdeacon of Liverpool. He was succeeded by Canon John W. Bardsley.

## 1887

On August 24th Canon John W. Bardsley, Archdeacon of Liverpool, was consecrated Bishop of Sodor and Man in York Minster. In 1892 Bishop Bardsley was translated to Carlisle where he served until 1904. He died in 1914 aged seventy nine years.

Bishop Ryle informed the Prime Minister, Lord Salisbury (1830/1903), of the importance of appointing an Archdeacon of Liverpool with whom, 'I can cordially co-operate'. The Revd William Lefroy, Vicar of St, Andrew's Church, Renshaw Street, Liverpool was appointed. He left in 1889 to become Dean of Norwich, where he served until his death in 1909. The Revd Benjamin Clarke, Vicar of Christ Church, Southport, succeeded him as Archdeacon of Liverpool.

To celebrate Queen Victoria's Golden Jubilee a Thanksgiving Service was held in the Pro-Cathedral. Many parishes in the Diocese celebrated the Queen's fifty year reign.

## 1889

In April Bishop Ryle's wife Henrietta died. She was buried in the churchyard of All Saints, Childwall.

On May 18th Bishop Ryle consecrated the Memorial Church of St Dunstan, Earle Road, Edge Hill. The church was founded by the Earle family to mark the spot where the family property originally stood. The Earle family played a major part in the early construction of the Cathedral.

Thomas Dyson Hornby (1822/1889), Chairman of the Mersey Docks Harbour Board, died in July. In 1905 his brother Henry Hugh Hornby a cotton broker, on behalf of the Hornby family, donated the *St Hilda and St Helena* window situated on the North side of the Lady Chapel.

The Revd William F. Taylor, Rural Dean of Walton, was appointed Archdeacon of Warrington.

## 1890

The first Liverpool branch of the Mothers Union was opened at St.Michael's Church, Garston. From the year 1900 branches were established worldwide.

# 1893

*Liverpool, which had been granted City status in 1880, was granted 'Mayoralty' and Robert Durning Holt (1832/1908), ship owner and local politician, became the first Lord Mayor of Liverpool.*

*Revd Francis James Chavasse*

*On April 25th St. Mark's Day, in a crowded York Minster, the Revd Francis James Chavasse was consecrated Bishop of Liverpool by the Archbishop of York the Most Revd William Maclagan.*

## 1891

Bishop Ryle established a 'Sustentation and Pension Fund' which gradually increased the incomes of clergy working in large parishes and allowed the older clergy to retire.

## 1892

Bishop Ryle appointed the Rt Revd Peter Sorenson Royston (1830/1915),who served as Bishop of Mauritius from 1872 to 1891, as Assistant Bishop. Bishop Royston returned to this country due to ill-health after thirty-five years of ministry in the Colonies. He served as Vicar of Childwall from 1896 to 1903.

## 1893

Liverpool, which had been granted City status in 1880, was granted 'Mayoralty' and Robert Durning Holt (1832/1908), ship owner and local politician, became the first Lord Mayor of Liverpool.

On May 23rd Bishop Ryle opened 'The Mary Clark Home' in Ullet Road, Liverpool. The Home, for elderly ladies' in reduced circumstances', was the gift of Mrs. Mary Clarke (1807/1887). Mary was the daughter of Robert Singlehurst, owner of the Red Cross shipping line. The Cathedral window in memory of Robert and his wife Hannah, in the South Choir aisle annexe, was destroyed in the Second World War and not replaced.

## 1894

Bishop Ryle initiated the 'Liverpool General Christian Mission' with the aim of halting the drift away from the church. During January and February every parish church in the Diocese took part in a nine day 'Mission'.

## 1895

The 16th Earl of Derby, who was to play a major role in promoting the building of the Cathedral, was elected Lord Mayor of Liverpool.

The Revd William F. Taylor was installed Archdeacon of Liverpool. He was succeeded as Archdeacon of Warrington by the Revd Thomas J. Madden, Vicar of St. Luke's Church, Liverpool.

## 1897

On June 20th, in the Pro-Cathedral, Bishop Ryle preached at a Diamond Jubilee Thanksgiving Service in celebration of Queen Victoria's long reign. All parish churches in the Diocese celebrated the occasion. To mark the event the parishioners of Christ Church, Bootle had placed in the tower a clock.

## 1898

On May 28th Bishop Ryle conducted a Memorial Service at St Nicholas Parish Church, Liverpool, for Mr. William Ewart Gladstone (1809/1898), the former Prime Minister, who died on May 19th at his family home in Hawarden. He is buried in Westminster Abbey. In 1881 Mr. Gladstone purchased the advowson of St Nicholas Church, Liverpool, from Liverpool Council, to ensure the appointment of Anglo-Catholic clergy.

## 1899

On August 1st Lady Constance Stanley (1840/1922), The Countess of Derby, laid the foundation stone of the Diocesan Church House. Bishop Ryle subscribed £1000 to the building and later bequeathed more than four thousand liturgical works for the formation of a library. The building, which was bombed during the Second World War, stood on the corner of Lord Street and South John Street.

The Liverpool Church Choir Association was formed to 'promote the study and practice of standard church music'.

The death was announced of Sir Richard Moon (1814/1899), Chairman of the London & North West Railway and promoter of the Mount Snowdon Railway. His name is inscribed on the marble flooring in the Eastern bay of the Choir, which was donated by his son Sir Ernest Moon (1854/1930) to his memory.

## 1900

Bishop Ryle announced his retirement and on March 3rd Lord Salisbury announced that he had the Queen's permission to offer the Revd Francis James Chavasse, Principal of Wycliffe Hall, Oxford, the Bishopric of Liverpool.

On April 25th St. Mark's Day, in a crowded York Minster, the Revd Francis James Chavasse was consecrated Bishop of Liverpool by the Archbishop of York the Most Revd William Maclagan (1826/1910). So large was the congregation that for the first time in the history of the Minster the ceremony of consecration took place not in the Choir but in the Nave. He was enthroned Bishop of Liverpool on May 31st in St Peter's Pro-Cathedral.

On June 10th Bishop Ryle, at the age of eighty three years, died at his home in Lowestoft, Suffolk, where he lived with his daughter Jessie Isabella. After his funeral service he was buried in the churchyard at All Saints, Childwall, Liverpool. In the Diocese he was affectionately known as 'the Working-Man's bishop'. During his episcopate he ordained 541 Priests and 535 Deacons. Confirmations increased from 4,000 to

# 1901

*On Tuesday January 22nd the death was announced of Queen Victoria (1819/1901). Public mourning commenced on January 24th and a Memorial Service for Her Majesty was held in the Pro-Cathedral.*

*Revd Francis James Chavasse and family.*

*A portrait of the young Queen Victoria is to be found in the Atrium window of the Lady Chapel.*

8,000 a year and during his ministry it was reported that as many as 134,000 young people were confirmed. Bishop Ryle's son Herbert Edward Ryle, who followed his father into the ministry, was Bishop of Exeter from 1900 to 1903, Bishop of Winchester 1903 to 1911 and Dean of Westminster from 1911 to 1925. On his death, Herbert was buried in Westminster Abbey close to the tomb of the unknown warrior which bears the inscription he composed.

On October 23rd Bishop Chavasse addressed the Diocesan Conference for the first time. Bishop Herbert Gresford Jones writing in *The Cathedral Builder* commented, 'it was evident that the building of a Cathedral was much upon his mind'.

Bishop Chavasse visited Formby for the first time on December 13th to preach at the newly opened Holy Trinity Church. The Bishop donated £50 to the Day School Building Fund (at this time the Vicar's stipend was £200 per annum).

## 1901

On Tuesday January 22nd the death was announced of Queen Victoria (1819/1901). Public mourning commenced on January 24th and a Memorial Service for Her Majesty was held in the Pro-Cathedral. The choral service, which was arranged by Canon Alexander Stewart, was led by Bishop Chavasse. Similar services took place throughout the Diocese. A portrait of the young Queen Victoria is to be found in the Atrium window of the Lady Chapel. She was succeeded by Edward V11.

Mr. George Hampson Morrison (1839/1901), an East India merchant of Liverpool, died on January 29th. In memory of her husband, Mrs. Morrison donated the marble flooring of the centre bay of the Choir and Steps of the Sanctuary. A memorial stone to his memory is situated on the North side of the Presbytery. His son's name, Alfred Hampson Clunie Morrison (1873/1910), is inscribed on the North side, at the base of the altar rail.

The marble flooring of the Western Bay of the Choir is in memory of Mr. Frank Rigby (1848/1919), a wine and spirit merchant, and was donated by the Trustees of F. Rigby.

On April 17th a Memorial Tablet, of Cipolino marble with sienna marble plasters, in memory of Bishop John C. Ryle was dedicated at St. Peters, the Pro-Cathedral.

The Sites' Committee presented a report with promises amounting to £125,000 for the building of a Cathedral.

On May 18th the first section of the Liverpool Diocesan Church House was opened by Archbishop Maclagan of York.

On Monday June 17th a Public Meeting at Liverpool Town Hall was convened by Bishop Chavasse and three resolutions were passed. The first, 'That the time has arrived when active steps should be taken to provide a Cathedral for the Diocese'. The second confirmed the adoption of the site on St James' Mount and the third constituted the Cathedral Committee. Bishop Chavasse reminded the meeting of why a Cathedral was needed, namely; 'The Cathedral would be a witness for God in the midst of this great city, the Cathedral was needed for diocesan and popular services, a Cathedral was needed to express and deepen the spiritual longings and aspirations of many among them'.

# 1902

*An Act of Parliament was obtained to authorise the acquisition of the site known as St James' Mount. The negotiations to acquire the site were led by Mr. Robert Hampson, secretary of the Cathedral Committee.*

*Mr. Hampson (1853/1919) was knighted by Edward VII on the day of the laying of the Cathedral's Foundation Stone.*

On June 21st Bishop Chavasse wrote to the parishes of the Diocese of the decision to build a Cathedral in which he expressed, 'that the effort must be great, united, sustained and with unceasing prayer'.

On June 24th the Executive Committee comprising of twenty four members was appointed by the Cathedral Committee. The committee met for the first time on the 1st of July.

On September 4th the Archdeacon of Warrington, the Revd Thomas Madden and Canon Tyrer recorded those who used the open space of St James' Mount between 5pm and 6pm. They recorded; '4 aged and decrepit men, 2 men like loafers or tramps, 2 disreputable looking women, 4 labourers, 5 children, 7 persons passing through'.

On September 16th, on the proposal of Sir William Bower Forwood, seconded by Sir Alfred L. Jones, it was unanimously resolved 'that St James' Mount be adopted as the site for the Cathedral. It was considered to be central and commanding and having picturesque surroundings'.

On September 23rd the Building Committee drew up conditions for the architectural competition. There was one specific condition that the designs were to be 'in the Gothic style'. In the face of much criticism from respected architects on October 28th this condition was rescinded and it was resolved that the question of style 'be left open'. In 1904 Giles Gilbert Scott wrote' Liverpool will have a Gothic Cathedral, but of quite a different type to that of our medieval Cathedrals; in fact, there is no Gothic building in the world to which it can be compared'.

Mr. George F. Bodley (1827/1907) and Mr. Norman Shaw (1831/1912) were appointed advisory architects to advise on the selection of an architect. The Cathedral Committee however reserved the right to make the final selection of an architect.

Bishop Chavasse inaugurated an annual 'Doctors' service at St Luke's Church, Liverpool on the Sunday nearest to St Luke's Day October 18th. The church, which was consecrated in 1831, was destroyed by an incendiary bomb on May 5th 1941. The burnt outer shell of the building is a reminder of the 'Liverpool Blitz' and the 'Garden of Remembrance' is a memorial to the Liverpool people who lost their lives in the Second World War.

The Revd Charles Harris (1861/1957) was appointed organizing secretary to the Cathedral Committee. He held the position until 1924 with the task of stimulating the interest of the Diocese in the Cathedral project by preaching and lecturing.

Mr. Frederick Morton Radcliffe (later Sir), solicitor, was appointed Treasurer. Frederick Radcliffe's father Sir David Radcliffe was born in Almondbury, Yorkshire, in 1834, the son of Amos Radcliffe a clothier. The family moved to Liverpool and David was apprenticed to an engineer and iron founder. Such was his success in business that he retired in 1882 to devote his life to public service, becoming the Mayor of Liverpool in 1884 and 1885. He was knighted in 1886 and appointed High Sheriff of Cheshire in 1892. Sir David died in 1907 and is buried in St. Mary's Churchyard, Knowsley. The left lancet of the *Church in England* window is to his memory. His son Frederick married Margaret Horsfall, the daughter of Alfred Horsfall, at St. Peter's Church, Formby in 1885. They had one son and four daughters.

Dr. A.W. Dale, Principal of University College, Liverpool, wrote to Bishop Chavasse dispelling the notion that the College was siding with the agitation against the cathedral scheme.

## 1902

On March 19th Noel and Christopher Chavasse were confirmed by their father Bishop Chavasse at St Saviour's Church, Falkner Square, Liverpool.

Architects were invited by public advertisement to submit portfolios of drawings by June. In July, one hundred and two portfolios of drawings for the preliminary competition were received. They were displayed at the Walker Art Gallery. Sir William Emmerson's original drawings for the Cathedral on the St John's Garden site were also displayed. To take part in a final competition Messrs Bodley and Shaw had the task to draw up a short list from the drawings that were received, Five architects, Messrs; Austin & Paley, C.A. Nicholson, M. Stark, W.J. Tapper and Giles Gilbert Scott were asked to submit full designs

On August 9th to mark the Coronation of King Edward VII a service was held in the Pro-Cathedral. Bishop Chavasse conducted the service which was attended by City councillors, Consuls and prominent people of Liverpool. As part of the celebrations, the Lord Mayor, Alderman Petrie hosted a meal for five hundred poor people in St George's Hall.

An Act of Parliament was obtained to authorise the acquisition of the site known as St James' Mount. The negotiations to acquire the site were led by Mr. Robert Hampson, secretary of the Cathedral Committee. As a result, an agreement with Liverpool Corporation was reached to purchase the land. In 1904, the year of his Mayorality, Mr. Hampson (1853/1919) was knighted by Edward VII on the day of the laying of the Cathedral's Foundation Stone. As one of the first officers of the Cathedral Committee his portrait appears in the *Laymen's* window.

# 1903

*On May 26th 1903
Mr Giles Gilbert Scott
was appointed architect.*

*George F Bodley (standing) and Giles
Gilbert Scott*

Mrs. C. Turner, in her will, bequeathed to the Bishopric Fund £10,000 and the same sum to the Cathedral Fund. In addition she left £25,000 to the Diocesan Fund for Incumbent Pensions.

The Liverpool Cathedral Act provided for the Bishop to act as Dean.

Mrs. Jane Lawrence (Earle) presented a crozier, the symbol of Episcopal jurisdiction, for the use of the Bishop of Liverpool.

The Cathedral Committee was reconstituted and Sir William Bower Forwood (1840/1928), ship owner and cotton broker, was appointed Chairman of the Executive Committee. Sir William was born at Edge Hill, Liverpool, the second son of Thomas Brittain Forwood (1810/1884) of Thornton Hough, Cheshire. His mother Charlotte Bower, was the daughter of William Bower, the founder of the firm William Bower and Sons, cotton brokers. Sir William Forwood's first wife, who died in 1896, was Mary Miles Morris the daughter of a Liverpool shipowner. They had three sons and seven daughters.

The Liverpool Cathedral Embroidery Association was formed; the Honorary Secretary was Miss Rosalie Stolterfoht. Lady Derby acted as President and Mrs. Chavasse and Mrs. Ireland Blackburne as Vice-Presidents. An oak cupboard to store the Altar frontals is dedicated to their memory.

## 1903

On May 26th Mr. Giles Gilbert Scott was appointed architect. Mr. George F. Bodley and Mr. R Norman Shaw, the assessors, in their final report wrote, 'We had to look for that power combined with beauty that makes a great and noble building. In the set of drawings by Mr.G.Gilbert Scott we find these qualities pre-eminently shown, we cannot but give it first place'.

In June the appointment was formally announced of Giles Gilbert Scott as architect with George F. Bodley as joint architect. All plans had to carry both their signatures.

On November 7th at St George's Hall the Lord Mayor Mr. W. Watson Rutherford presented the Charter of the University of Liverpool to the 16th Earl of Derby, the first Chancellor of the University. The Arms of the University are to be found in the West clerestory window in the South East transept, alongside those of the Earl of Derby.

Miss E. Brancker of Wells, Somerset, contributed the sum of £800 towards the cost of the font (erected in 1944). Also, with her brother, Mr. Charles Brancker, she donated the Lady Chapel window which depicts

*St Non and St Bride,* in memory of their parents John and Mary Brancker. John Brancker (1818/1903) was a Liverpool produce broker and was Chairman of the Mersey Docks and Harbour Board from 1890 to 1899. For over two hundred years the Brancker family played a prominent role in the civic and commercial life of the city. Benjamin Brancker in the 18th century worked as a Silversmith in the city. His work is now much sought after. His grandson Peter Whitfield Brancker was Mayor of Liverpool in 1801 and Sir Thomas Brancker was Mayor in 1831.

*The Liverpool Diocesan Gazette,* which contained a monthly record of diocesan work, was published for the first time at a cost of one penny. *The Gazette* was edited by the Revd Charles Harris, Vicar of Christ Church, Newburgh, Wigan.

Messrs. Northcroft, Neighbour & Nicholson of Liverpool were appointed as quantity surveyors.

The death occurred of the Revd Samuel Ashton Thompson Yates (1843/1903). He was general benefactor of Liverpool University College and donor of the Thompson Yates laboratories situated in the Quadrangle (off Ashton Street) Liverpool. The Lady Chapel window, which depicts *St Margaret of Antioch and St Ethereda,* was donated by his nephews and nieces in memory of their uncle.

As a result of the generosity of the 16th Earl of Derby, Sir Alfred Jones and others the St James' Mount site was purchased from Liverpool Corporation. The houses situated on the site were also purchased and the final cost of acquiring the site was £19,424.

## 1904

By the beginning of the year more than £180,000, consisting of small sums as well as large, had been subscribed to the Building Fund. The Executive Committee decided that before the 'Foundation Stone' be laid, the contributions should amount to not less than £200,000. The committee estimated the cost of building the Cathedral to be in excess of £500,000.

On July 19th King Edward VII laid the 'Foundation Stone', and in a loud and sonorous voice declared; ' In the name of the Father, Son and Holy Ghost I declare this stone well and truly laid'. The trowel and mallet, the gift of Elkington & Co, used for the laying of the stone were handed to the King by the young architect Giles Gilbert Scott. The implements later became prized exhibits at the Church Congress and Ecclesiastical Art Exhibition held in Brighton later in the year. The mallet and trowel used by King Edward VII, when laying the 'Foundation Stone', were returned to the Cathedral and in June 1975 the mallet was used by Bishop David Sheppard to gain entry to the

# 1905

*Dr. Frederick H. Burstall, who conducted the massed choirs of the Liverpool Church Choir Association at the laying of the Foundation Stone, was appointed organist.*

Cathedral for his installation as Bishop of Liverpool.

The 'Foundation Stone' from Runcorn Hill quarry, inscribed by the sculptor George Herbert Tyson Smith (1883/1972), was presented by the Mothers' Meetings of the Diocese and cost £90. The stone which weighs five and a half ton is seven foot ten inches long, four foot six inches wide, and two foot four inches deep.

The Service for laying of the 'Foundation Stone' was conducted by Archbishop Maclagan of York who consecrated the stone. The Archbishop was assisted by Bishop Chavasse and Bishop Francis Jayne (1845/1921) respectively Bishops of Liverpool and Chester.

Dr. Frederick H. Burstall, who conducted the massed choirs of the Liverpool Church Choir Association, at the laying of the foundation stone, was appointed organist. The Mustel organ, played by Mr. Charles Collins at the ceremony, was presented to the Cathedral by Dr. Burstall's great nephew John Burstall, and is situated in the Lady Chapel.

In November Mr. Arthur Earle, on behalf of the Earle and Langton families, donated £25,000 for the erection of the Lady Chapel.

On November 12th Bishop Chavasse attended the opening of the Medical School and George Holt Physics Laboratory at Liverpool University.

Mr. A. Green was appointed Clerk of Works at a salary of £5 a week. A week later, on the recommendation of the architect, it was raised to £6 a week.

On the proposition of Bishop Chavasse the title of the Cathedral was to be 'The Cathedral Church of Christ'.

The Executive Committee resolved, 'That it should be a requirement that, except in special circumstances, it was desirable that the privilege of providing windows or other special gifts for the Cathedral be accorded only where these are offered in memory of a subscriber of a substantial sum to the building fund'.

Mrs. Barrow's offer of £10,000, in memory of her husband Mr. James Barrow, to defray the cost of providing the Cathedral with an organ, was accepted by the Executive Committee.

## 1905

On January 23rd the responsibilities of the Building Committee were transferred to the Executive Committee.

The offer of a window in the Lady Chapel, to be placed over the main entrance, was declined on the advice of the architects as it would spoil, 'one of the best bits of the Chapel design'.

The Gladstone Memorial Committee offered the sum of £600 to defray the cost of a window in memory of William Ewart Gladstone, M.P. (1809/1898). In accepting the gift the Executive Committee put on record their pleasure, 'that the memory of a statesman of his eminence and noble character should be perpetuated in the Cathedral of his native city'. The St Mark window on the South side of the Choir is to his memory. A portrait of his wife Mrs. Catherine Gladstone (1812/1896) is to be found in the Atrium window in The Lady Chapel.

*The Mustel Organ played at the laying of the Foundation Stone in 1904.*

# 1906

*On July 17th the Most Worshipful Grand Master, H.R.H. The Duke of Connaught and Strathearn (brother of King Edward VII) laid the 'Foundation Stone' of the Chapter House.*

Miss Mary Leicester donated the St Luke window in memory of her father the Revd Robert Leicester (1799/1875) the Rector of St Peter's, Woolton. In 1826 he was the first incumbent of the Chapel-of Ease to Childwall, which served the newly formed parish of St Peter's. The present Church was consecrated by Bishop Ryle in 1887.

Colonel Henry B.H. Blundell (1831/1906) donated the Lady Chapel window which depicts *St Perpetua and St Cecilia.* His brother the Revd Thomas Blundell, Rector of Halsall, was Chaplain to Bishop Ryle and Honorary Chaplain to Queen Victoria. Their ancestor Bryan Blundell (1674/1756) was the founder of the Bluecoat Hospital and in the original window, at its base, the name 'Blundell' was supported by a Bluecoat boy and girl. It is believed that the model for the portrait of the Bluecoat girl was that of a girl from Woolton Village. Bryan Blundell's portrait appears in the fourth lancet of the *Te Deum* window.

Captain Henry Heywood Lonsdale D.S.O (1864/1930) donated the Lady Chapel window which depicts *St Catherine and St Lucy* in memory of the Lonsdale family. Henry, who served with the Grenadier Guards, was the son of Arthur Pemberton Heywood Lonsdale (1835/1897) of Shavington Hall, Market Rasen, Shropshire. Henry's grandfather, the Revd Henry Glyby Lonsdale (1791/ 1851) was Vicar of St Mary's, Lichfield.

which were to be of stone. The committee also approved Giles Gilbert Scott's plan for much taller windows with only two lights.

The first design for a Lady Chapel festal frontal was received. It was the work of Mrs. Phoebe Powell, wife of Canon Frank J. Powell, Vicar of St John the Evangelist, Knotty Ash. The Revd Powell was vicar of St John for 54 years, from 1885 to 1939.

A model, in pear wood, of the proposed Cathedral was exhibited. It was made by Mr. L. A. Turner under the direction of the architects Messrs Bodley and Scott, and commissioned by the Building Committee.

The Rt Revd Peter Royston, Assistant Bishop, retired.

The Diocese presented Bishop Chavasse with a car.

## 1906

The foundations of the Choir, Lady Chapel and Chapter House were completed in April.

On May 14th the Executive Committee instructed the firm of Morrison & Sons of Wavertree, Liverpool to proceed with the super-structure. Stone from the Woolton quarry, owned by Lord Salisbury (1861/1947), being selected for this work.

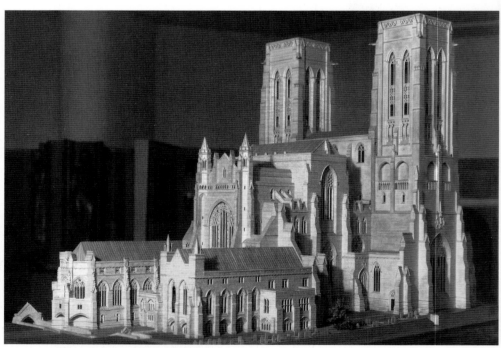

*A model, in pear wood, of the proposed Cathedral was exhibited. It was made by Mr. L. A. Turner under the direction of the architects Messrs Bodley and Scott, and commissioned by the Building Committee.*

Mrs. Myers donated the Lady Chapel window which depicts *St Agnes and St Faith* in memory of her husband Canon Charles Myers, who was born in Liverpool. He served as Rector of St Martins, New Sarum, Wiltshire and as Canon of Salisbury Cathedral.

The Executive Committee decided that the roof of the Lady Chapel be groined in concrete except for the ribs

Morrison & Sons in 1901 completed the building of the Stanley tobacco warehouse in Liverpool which, at that time, was the largest brick building in the world, 27 million bricks being used for its construction. The total number of bricks used in the construction of the Cathedral is estimated between 12 and 13 million.

On July 17th the Most Worshipful Grand Master,

# 1907

*On October 21st the death occurred, at the age of eighty years, of Mr. George Frederick Bodley the joint architect.*

*Mr. George Frederick Bodley the joint architect.*

H.R.H. The Duke of Connaught and Strathearn (brother of King Edward VII) laid the 'Foundation Stone' of the Chapter House. The Chapter House was the gift of the Province of West Lancashire in memory of the first Earl of Lathom, Edward Bootle Wilbraham (1837/1898). Edward, who was known as Lord Skelmersdale, was a Conservative politician and a member of every Conservative administration between 1866 and 1898, serving three times as Lord Chamberlain. His portrait and that of his son Edward Bootle Wilbraham (1864/1910) appear in the North window of the Chapter House.

On July 19th the Executive Committee agreed to assign the Lady Chapel porch to the children of the Diocese as their special gift and ordained that all children's offerings be earmarked for this purpose.

In September to celebrate Bishop Chavasse's sixtieth birthday, and his and Mrs. Chavasse's silver wedding, the clergy of the Diocese presented him with a gift of silver plate and an English clock with cathedral chimes.

The Revd Thomas J. Madden, Vicar of St Luke's Church, Liverpool succeeded the Revd William F. Taylor as Archdeacon of Liverpool.

The Revd George Hardwicke Spooner, Rector of Walton-on-the-Hill, was installed Archdeacon of Warrington. The offer to present the Choir Stalls by Mr. S. J. Waring senior (1860/1940), father of the first Lord Waring, was accepted by the Executive Committee.

Mr. Howard Douglas Horsfall's (1857/1936) gift of a reredos costing £5,000 was declined. Mr. Horsfall who had been a member of the Executive Committee from 1901 resigned. He was the founder and benefactor of St Faiths Church, Great Crosby, St Agnes Church, Liverpool and St Chads Theological College in Durham.

Mr. G.F. Bodley, the joint architect, was appointed as architect for the new Cathedral in Washington, U.S.A.

## 1907

In January the 'Bishop of Liverpool's Fund' was established.

On August 3rd 'The Liverpool Pageant' was held to celebrate the 700th anniversary of the granting of the Town's Charter (in 1207 King John granted *Letters Patent* and in 1229 his son Henry III gave Liverpool a Charter constituting it a free Borough). Mr. Frederick H. Burstall the Cathedral organist composed the music to William Watson's *Anniversary Ode.*

On October 21st the death occurred, at the age of

eighty years, of Mr. George Frederick Bodley the joint architect. He is recognised as the most influential designer of the 'Gothic Revival' in the last quarter of the nineteenth century. He is buried in the Churchyard of St James Parish Church, Kinnersley, Herefordshire. As one of the joint architects his portrait appears in the *Laymen's* window.

On November 7th Mr. Giles Gilbert Scott became the sole architect.

The death occurred of Mr. Robert Morrison senior partner in the firm of the builders of the Cathedral. Two windows on the North side of the Lady Chapel, depicting *St Osburga and St Frydeswyde, St Werburga and St Bega,* are to his memory.

Mr. Cecil Greenwood Hare (1875/1932), the architect and designer, was appointed designer of Cathedral embroideries. He designed the Altar festal burse which was made during the First World War by the Cathedral Embroidery Association.

The Executive Committee accepted the offer of the Earle family for a window in memory of Sir Thomas Earle (1820/1900) and his wife Dame Emily Earle (1832/1905). Sir Thomas Earle who was Mayor of Liverpool in 1853 is buried with his wife in St Peter's Churchyard, Woolton. The St John window on the South side of the Choir is to their memory. The original window was destroyed in the Second World War and replaced in 1947. It was the last Cathedral window to be designed by James Hogan.

## 1908

On February 7th James Powell & Sons (Whitefriars) submission of four cartoons for the Lady Chapel windows was accepted by the Stained Glass sub-committee. The Revd John Augustine Kempthorne (1846/1946) and Mr. Frederick M. Radcliffe had responsibility for the selection of subjects for the Lady Chapel windows. The Revd Kempthorne was Rector of St Nicholas Church, Liverpool, and Honorary Canon at the Cathedral. He was later appointed Bishop of Hull (1910/1913) and Bishop of Lichfield (1913/1937). The windows were designed and drawn by James W. Brown (1842/1928). The painting of the glass, including that of the portraits, was the work of A. A. Burcombe of Whitefriars Studios. These windows were badly damaged in 1941 and replaced by the present windows.

On April 6th the Executive Committee accepted the offer of Mr. F. Tobin to give a rose window entitled, *The Sea,* at the East end of the South Choir aisle in memory of his father James Aspinall Tobin (1819/1891), who had been a palm oil trader. He was Mayor of Liverpool 1854/1855 and a member of the Mersey Docks Harbour Board, being in attendance at

# 1909

*The windows in the Lady Chapel were completed and fixed. The cost of all the windows amounted to £4000.*

*On June 14th the death occurred of the Frederick Arthur Stanley, 16th Earl of Derby (1841/1908), the first President of the Cathedral Committee. As one of the original members of the committee his portrait features in the Laymen's window.*

the first meeting of the Board on January 5th 1858.

The rose window entitled, *Missions,* at the East end of the North Choir aisle was the gift of Mrs. Chambers, in memory of her husband Lt-Col. Francis Herbert Chambers of Seaforth, Lancashire.

Bishop Chavasse welcomed 120 German visitors to the Pro-Cathedral on May 31st.

On June 14th the death occurred of the Frederick Arthur Stanley, 16th Earl of Derby (1841/1908), the first President of the Cathedral Committee. As one of the original members of the committee his portrait features in the *Laymen's* window. The 16th Earl is buried at St Mary's Church, Knowsley. He was succeeded by his son Edward George Villiers Stanley.

In July Bishop Chavasse attended the Lambeth Conference in London, which was presided over by the Archbishop of Canterbury the Most Revd Randall Davidson (1848/1930). The Archbishop was present at the consecration of the Cathedral in 1924 but took no part in the actual ceremony. His portrait appears in The *Bishops'* window alongside Bishop Chavasse.

On October 10th at St Peter's the Pro-Cathedral, Bishop Chavasse's daughter Dorothea married the Revd George Foster-Carter (1876/1966), Rector of St. Aldate's, Oxford and Bishop Chavasse's examining Chaplain. They had two children, Aymler Francis (1911/1979) and Pamela Mary (1918/1967).

Mr. A.W. Bibby, Chairman of the Pacific Steam Navigation Co, presented to the Cathedral an oil painting by the portrait artist John Rogers Herbert (1810/1890) entitled, *Acquital of the Seven Bishops.* The right lancet of the *Bishops'* window depicts the seven Bishops who were imprisoned and tried over their opposition to the second 'Declaration of Indulgence' issued by James II in 1688. The lancet is in memory of Archibald James Tod (1851/1927) and Alice Jane Lucy Tod(1858/1946). The left lancet is in memory of James Stephen Walmsley Shaw (1831/1907), a furnishing Iron Monger (Master), and Margaret Shaw (1836/1908). The window was the gift of their daughter Miss Florence Shaw (1871/1948). The family lived in West Derby, Liverpool.

The offer of the gift of a Processional Cross was declined by Bishop Chavasse.

The 17th Earl of Derby (1865/1948) was elected as President of the Cathedral Committee and the 2nd Lord Lathom (1864/1910) as Vice-President.

The death occurred, at his home 2 Rodney Street, Liverpool, of the Liverpool surgeon Dr. Edward Robert Bickersteth (1828/1908). The son of Dr. Robert and Katherine Bickersteth he was born in 1828 at

2 Rodney Street. He was President of the Medical Institution in 1870 and President of the surgical section of the British Medical Association in 1883. He was one of the first to appreciate and make use of the antiseptic system of using carbolic acid which had been adopted by his friend and former fellow student Joseph Lister (1827/1912) the pioneer of antiseptic surgery. Although the family home remained at 2 Rodney Street Edward owned an estate at Craig-y-don, Anglesey, from where during the summer months he sailed his yacht. A window (the right lancet), to his memory was donated by his widow Anne in 1910. At her request the window was to be sited as near as possible to his burial place in St James' cemetery. Her wish was granted when The *Scholars'* window was erected nearly fifty years after his death. In 1995, to allow for new drains to be laid in the cemetery, Dr. Bickersteth's gravestone was relocated to the edge of the car park overlooking the cemetery and so nearer to the window.

The left lancet of *The Scholars'* window was the gift of L. Loxdale Murray, in memory of his father George Loxdale Murray (1834/1906) and his grandfather Henry Murray (1801/1864). At the request of the family the window was sited as near as possible to their burial place in St. James' cemetery.

Forest of Dean stone was selected for the construction of the canopies on the Children's Porch. However twenty years later, due to erosion, the canopies had to be cut away.

## 1909

By April 1st the walls of the Lady Chapel had reached their full height of 55 feet.

The windows in the Lady Chapel were completed and fixed. The cost of all the windows amounted to £4000.

In December the death occurred of Sir Alfred Jones (1844/1909), a colonial produce broker, at his home 'Oaklands', Aigburth. He was a member of the Executive Committee from 1901, a generous donor to the Cathedral Building Fund, and founder of the Liverpool School of Tropical Medicine. In his memory his sister Mrs. Pinnock gave a gift of £1000 for the St Matthew window which is situated in the North Choir aisle. In 1913 a memorial of Sir Alfred, situated at the Pierhead, was unveiled by the 17th Earl of Derby. The memorial takes the form of a tall and slender granite pedestal with two projecting base courses. On top of the pedestal is a bronze allegorical female figure, representing Liverpool. In her left hand is a model of a ship upon a globe, whilst her right hand is slightly extended 'welcoming Commerce to the Port of Liverpool'. Two seated allegorical figures on the base course represent 'The

# 1910

*On Friday May 6th the death of King Edward V11 was announced.*

*On March 16th Bishop Chavasse wrote to Dr. Montague Butler (1833/1918) requesting an authentic portrait of Josephine Butler (1828/1906) the social reformer, to serve as a model for a stained glass window in the Lady Chapel.*

Fruits of Industry' and 'Research', alluding to Sir Alfred.

Messrs. Rattee and Kent's of Cambridge tender of £700 for the making of the Lady Chapel Reredos was accepted. The Reredos, jointly designed by the architects Bodley and Scott, was carved by the sculptor and artist Mr. Alfred Southwick (1875/1944). The Reredos was the gift of Mrs. Eleanor H. Gilmour in memory of her parents Joseph Langton (1792/1855) and Ann Langton (1798/1875), daughter of Thomas Earle (1755/1822) of Spekelands, Liverpool. Joseph Langton was the first manager of the Bank of Liverpool. Eleanor Gilmour also donated the Apse windows in the Lady Chapel which depict; *the Annunciation, the Adoration of the Magi, and the Presentation in the Temple,* in memory of her husband Hamilton Boswell Gilmour an East Indian merchant. The family crest, *Nil Penna Sed Usus* (Not the quill but its use) also appears in the window. The altar and ornaments were donated by Mrs. Langton in memory of her husband and children. Mrs. Gertrude Langton gave the vases for the altar. The Misses Langton defrayed the cost of the marble flooring in the Lady Chapel Sanctuary in memory of Charles Langton. The remainder of the green Swedish marble flooring was donated by Miss Langton and Mrs. Langton as a memorial to the Langton family.

Miss Stolterfoht, Hon. Secretary of the Cathedral Embroidery Association, provided all the frontals, fine linen, hangings, alms bags, surplices and kneelers for the Lady Chapel.

The red frontal for the Lady Chapel altar was donated by six ladies from Mossley Hill. Mrs. Florence Ismay, wife of the shipping magnate Bruce Ismay, who was one of the donors and embroiderers stitched one of the stars. The green frontal for the Lady Chapel altar was designed by George Bodley and produced by Miss Margaret Comber who was considered to be the most prolific and skilful of the embroiderers.

Rather than the original rectangular design the Executive Committee decided to adopt a smaller octagonal design for the Chapter House. Accordingly, the architect was asked to redesign the Chapter House.

The Girls' Friendly Society of the Diocese gave a gift of £200 for the windows in the Atrium and on the staircase of the Lady Chapel. Referred to as 'the Noble Women' windows they depict, in 23 glass panels, women who have had a major influence on society locally and nationally, and who were much admired in the period 1904 to 1910 when the Lady Chapel was being built. Bishop Chavasse wrote of those portrayed in the window, 'women who have made the world a better place'. The Girls' Friendly Society was established in 1875 by Mary Elizabeth Townsend to protect young working girls.

The city witnessed many weeks of Protestant-Catholic violence, often inflamed by religious pageantry and inflammatory oratory.

# 1910

On February 20th Bishop Chavasse ordained his son Christopher at St Bride's Church, Catharine Street, Liverpool.

On March 16th Bishop Chavasse wrote to Dr. Montague Butler (1833/1918) requesting an authentic portrait of Josephine Butler (1828/1906) the social reformer, to serve as a model for a stained glass window in the Lady Chapel. Dr. Butler, Josesphine's brother-in-law, sent the Bishop a copy of W.T. Stead's *A Life Sketch of Josephine Butler.* However, Bishop Chavasse chose George Richmond's (1809/1896) drawing of 1851, which was the frontispiece of George and Lucy Johnson's 1909 book entitled, *Autobiographical Memoir of Josephine Butler.*

On Friday May 6th the death of King Edward VII was announced. He was succeeded by King George V.

On Tuesday June 28 the last of the week-day Cathedral services was held in the Pro-Cathedral.

On St Peter's Day Wednesday June 29th at 11.00 am, in the presence of the Most Revd Cosmo Lang Archbishop of York, the Consecration of the Lady Chapel took place. The Archbishop for his sermon took as his text Habakkuk 2;20 'The Lord is in his holy temple'. Dr. Frederick H. Burstall presided at the organ. A ten year old choir boy named Arthur Askey (1900/1982), who later became a well known comedian, sang solo *'On the wings of a dove'.* As a memento each chorister was presented with a silver casket. In 1981 Mr. D. Shadrach, one of the choristers, presented to the Cathedral the silver casket he had received with a collection of other memorabilia.

The Lady Chapel organ was built by Henry Willis and Sons and presented in memory of Elizabeth and Georgina, daughters of Sir Hardman Earle (1792/1877), a director of the Liverpool to Manchester Railway. Earlestown, is named after him.

The organ case was designed by Giles Gilbert Scott. The sculptured stone figures of angels above the organ gallery were given in memory of James Dickson Dixon and his wife Elizabeth by Mrs. Phoebe Powell and her sister.

The estimated cost of the Lady Chapel, described by the architect 'as a free interpretation of 14th century Gothic', was £70,000, with the Earle and Langton families contributing nearly one-half of the cost. On October 3rd the architect submitted a proposal and drawings to alter the original design of the

# 1912

*During April, Memorial Services were held in the Pro- Cathedral and the Lady Chapel for those who lost their lives in the sinking of the RMS Titanic.*

*Carving of the RMS Titanic by James Dilworth.*

*Mr. Thomas Bartlett (1839/1912) of 6 Pembroke Place, a Liverpool wine and spirit merchant and the donor of the bells, died on September 4th 1912.*

Cathedral in a manner which he thought 'would add to the architectural effect of the building and would provide a large central space for great popular services'. At the November meeting the proposal was accepted in principle by the Executive Committee. The architect had first mooted this change to the design of the Cathedral in 1909.

Under the Cathedral Act of 1902 Bishop Chavasse became the Acting Dean. He appointed Canon Harold E. Bilborough, Rector of Liverpool, as Sub- Dean.

Bishop Chavasse informed the architect that the inscriptions on the wings of the Lady Chapel Reredos, 'To be in English and not Latin and to be written in letters which all may read'.

A silver alms dish and altar vessels for use in the Lady Chapel were presented by Miss Neilson and Mr. R.N. Neilson. They were designed and made by Messrs Lambert, gold and silversmiths, of Coventry Street, London. The sedilia were presented by Mrs. Moss, in memory of Gilbert Moss and by Miss Oakshott on behalf of the 'Ladies of Wirral'. Two silver gilt patens were presented by the children of Thomas and Mary Moss.

The Bishop's Mace (The Gold Mace), executed by Bainbridge Reynolds, was presented by Miss Robinson in memory of her brother Alfred Robinson. The head of the mace, at the suggestion of the architect, was remodelled in 1932. Miss Robinson also presented the Chapter Mace.

Mr. Joseph Harrod was appointed Head Verger.

The death occurred of Mr. Thomas Sutton Timmis (1830/1910), a soap and chemical manufacturer and partner in the firm Gossage & Sons, soap makers of Widnes. He was a member of the Executive Committee from 1903. *The Spirit of Service* window, situated in the Derby transept, is in memory of Thomas and his wife Caroline Anne (1830/1903). The marble flooring of the Sanctuary and platform of the Holy Table is also to their memory and their grandson 2nd Lieut. Richard Sutton Timmis of the Kings Royal Rifle Corps, who died in the First World War. In addition Mr. Timmis initiated a trust fund for the maintenance of the Cathedral services with a gift of £1000. The family were generous benefactors to numerous schemes in Liverpool which included, in 1903, a gift of £10,000 to the Royal Hospital to assist in the research of the causes of cancer.

## 1911

In August the Liverpool transport strike led to industrial unrest throughout the city. Morrison, the builders of the Cathedral, expressed their concern 'that

there might, in the present condition of labour, be a strike with a demand for some considerable increase such as 1d. (one old pence) an hour which would mean an addition of about 10 per cent to the wages'. On August 13th, during the protests in Liverpool, a docker and carter were shot dead by troops. The day became known as 'Bloody Sunday'.

Mrs. Agnes Wood gave £10,000 to the building fund to provide the Reredos in the Choir. The gift was in memory of her husband James Marke Wood the Liverpool shipping line owner.

The Revd Charles Harris' book, *The Building of the New Liverpool Cathedral,* was published.

## 1912

During April, Memorial Services were held in the Pro- Cathedral and the Lady Chapel for those who lost their lives in the sinking of the RMS *Titanic.* A stone carving of the *Titanic,* by James Townley Dilworth of Liverpool, is to be found on the East end gallery situated in the North Choir aisle.

Mr. Thomas Bartlett (1839/1912) of 6 Pembroke Place, a Liverpool wine and spirit merchant and the donor of the bells, died on September 4th. He was the son of John Adam Bartlett (1786/1855), a Devon shipowner, who moved to Liverpool at the turn of the 19th century to take advantage of the growing importance of the port of Liverpool. Thomas's ashes lie in a casket situated over the door to the Ringing Chamber. His brother William Bartlett (1837/1917) was an original member of the Cathedral Building Committee. Their parents John and Mary Bartlett are buried in St Mary's Churchyard, Edge Hill, Liverpool.

As a result of the generosity of Mrs. Barrow, the widow of James Barrow the Liverpool provision dealer, the contract to build the Cathedral organ was placed with Henry Willis and Sons Ltd. The Liverpool Branch of the Organ Builders' Trade Society wrote to the Bishop suggesting that the organ be built in Liverpool.

The second section of the Diocesan Church House was opened by Archbishop Cosmo Lang, of York.

## 1913

From May 1st the wages of bricklayers, joiners and masons went up from ten 'old' pence to ten and half 'old' pence per hour. Labourers received six 'old' pence per hour.

During November and December attacks on property by militant suffragettes occurred across the city and included a peaceful demonstration in the Lady Chapel when banners were waved and leaflets were thrown from the gallery during Matins.

# 1914

*The First World War commenced on August 4th. For the following six years the building of the Cathedral was severely disrupted.*

On December 10th Her Majesty Queen Alexandra (1844/1925) made an unofficial visit to the Cathedral to see how the building work was progressing. After the death of her husband, Edward VII in 1910, she devoted her life to charitable work. One such cause being Alexandra Rose Day (June 26th), when artificial roses produced by people with disabilities were sold to raise funds for hospitals.

Sir William Bower Forwood (1840/1928), Chairman of the Executive Committee, resigned. He was succeeded by Mr. Frederick Morton Radcliffe (later Sir Radcliffe).

Mr. Arthur Earle made a gift of £10,000 to the Building Fund which he had offered in 1910, provided that £50,000 was raised before 1915.

An annual diocesan budget was made.

The contract with Messrs Powell for the Great East window *(Te Deum)* was approved. The cost of £4,200 was met by the executors of Mrs. Margaret Ismay (1837/1907), the widow of Thomas Henry Ismay (1837/1899) who founded The White Star shipping company. In her will she directed that her executors, 'endeavour to secure that both in design and execution it shall be as perfect as may be'. In addition, Mrs. Ismay subscribed £10,000 to the Building Fund.

The list of names for the *Te Deum* window was agreed. As representatives of Christian soldiers the name of Sir Philip Sydney (1554/1586), the poet and soldier, was replaced in the fourth lancet, entitled *The Holy Church throughout the World,* by Field Marshall Frederick Roberts (1832/1914),V.C., who with his son Lieutenant Frederick Roberts (1872/1899),V.C., were

*An Altar festal frontal, designed by Cecil Greenwood Hare, was completed by the Cathedral Embroidery Association. The piece, which contains 35 figures, was the work of Margaret Comber and Josephine Chambres. Hare stated, 'it was the best amateur work he had ever seen'.*
*It was donated by Caroline August Best in memory of Thomas Best. Caroline also donated the four sculpted angels in the choir.*

one of only three pairs of fathers and sons to be awarded the Victoria Cross.

A request by Sir Foster Cunliffe (1875/1916) that a monument of his ancestor, the Liverpool merchant Sir Ellis Cunliffe (1717/1767), who had been a Member of Parliament for Liverpool, be moved from St. Peter's Pro-Cathedral to the Cathedral was declined.

The Revd Christopher Chavasse became Chaplain to his father Bishop Chavasse.

An Altar festal frontal, designed by Cecil Greenwood Hare, was completed by the Cathedral Embroidery Association. The piece, which contains 35 figures, was the work of Margaret Comber and Josephine Chambres. Hare stated, 'it was the best amateur work he had ever seen'.

## 1914

The First World War commenced on August 4th. For the following six years the building of the Cathedral was severely disrupted. The number of men employed, which for the eight years prior to 1914 had averaged 243, dropped for the next six years to an average of 60, and the quarries were not fully operational again until 1920.

On August 7th Dr. Mary Birrell Davies established the Liverpool Women's War Service Bureau at 1, Gambier Terrace. The bureau was organised by women and its committee included many of the women whose families had a close association with the Cathedral. The object of the bureau was to assist and help the families of Liverpool soldiers and sailors.

# 1915

*On Friday May 7th the Cunard liner RMS Lusitania was sunk by a German U-Boat, U20, off the coast of Ireland.*

*Miss Lillie Reed, Sculptress.*

In August the death occurred of Mr. James Crofts Powell (1847/1914). He was a member of the Powell family whose firm, known as WhiteFriars Glass, produced many of the Cathedral windows. James and his cousin Harry Powell developed new forms, colours and decorative techniques, in addition to creating special industrial glass for scientific uses.

On September 2nd Giles Gilbert Scott married Louise Wallbank Hughes at the Church of Saint Cecilia, Kingsway, London. Louise worked as a receptionist at the Adelphi Hotel where Giles stayed on his visits to Liverpool.

The Anglican Church in Wales was disestablished on September 18th.

In November, in view of the policy of war-time economy, the salary of the Revd Charles Harris, the Cathedral Committee's organising secretary, was reduced from £100 per annum to £50 per annum

The Society of Operative Stonemasons' offer to work shorter hours was accepted by the Executive Committee.

The carvings of the figures on the Children's Porch were completed. The figures by the sculptress Miss Lillie Reed (1875/1948) depict Christ as The Good Shepherd with two children, David with a sling, Samuel with a temple lamp, Timothy with a roll of the Scriptures and the boy with loaves and fishes. The one looking on the Founders' Plot is the boy King Josiah. To put the finishing touches to her work she was hoisted aloft on a crane. The sculpture for the Children's Porch and for the porch itself was partly met by the donations of the children of the Diocese. Miss Reed was born in London and studied sculpture at the Slade school. She exhibited on several occasions at the Royal Academy.

Mr. Henry Heywood Noble, who had served on the Executive Committee from 1912, succeeded Sir Arthur Stanley as Honorary Treasurer.

Sir William Forwood donated the pulpit in memory of his brother Sir Arthur Forwood M.P. (1836/1898) and Mr. John Torr M.P.(1813/1886) who were instrumental in raising the fund for the endowment of the See of Liverpool.

The Singlehurst family's offer of £500 for a window in memory of Mr. and Mrs. Robert Singlehurst was accepted by the Executive Committee. Mr. Singlehurst who was a Liverpool shipowner died in 1912. The Cathedral window to their memory was situated in the South Choir aisle annexe. The window, which contained the coat of arms of the See of Winchester and the See of Lincoln, was destroyed in the Second World War. The Singlehurst family were the main benefactors of St Barnabas Parish Church which was

consecrated by Bishop Chavasse on February 21st 1914.

The offer by the Church choirs of the Diocese to raise £500 to provide suitable gates to the Choir area was accepted by the Executive Committee. At this time it was intended that there should be a screen across the Choir Arch. This scheme was subsequently abandoned. However it is possible to identify one or two stones about a third of the way up the piers of the arch which are lighter in colour than the other stones. These were originally the springers of the screen arch and were trimmed down shortly before the Cathedral was consecrated.

## 1915

The year marked the 700th anniversary of the signing of the *Magna Carta.* Cardinal Stephen Langton, Archbishop of Canterbury, the first signatory on the document, is depicted in the *Church in England* window. He is also depicted in the *Te Deum* window.

Lt. Thomas H. Madden of the Duke of Cornwall Light Infantry was fatally wounded at Neuve Chapple, France, on May 3rd. He was the son of the Revd Thomas Madden, Archdeacon of Liverpool and Vicar of Christ Church, Southport. A stained glass window erected in St Luke's Church, Liverpool, and dedicated by Bishop Chavasse to his memory, was destroyed when the church was bombed in the Second World War.

On Friday May 7th the Cunard liner RMS *Lusitania* was sunk by the German U-Boat, U20, off the coast of Ireland. One thousand one hundred and ninety eight people lost their lives. Many of the crew who lost their lives were from Liverpool. Memorial Services took place throughout the Diocese. Many of the names of those who lost their lives are recorded in the Cathedral's 'Roll of Honour'. The *Lusitania* sailed from Liverpool on her maiden voyage to New York on the 7th September 1907, watched by over 200,000 people.

On May 10th 2nd Lt. Richard Sutton Timmis, of the Kings Royal Rifle Corps, aged 19 years, died of the wounds he received in action near Ypres. He is buried at Bailleul Community Cemetery. The Baptistery window was given by his parents Henry Sutton Timmis and Annie Timmis to his memory. His name is also recorded on the family gravestone at Toxteth Park Cemetery, Liverpool.

The Choir stalls of English oak, the gift of Lord S.J.Waring (1860/1940) and Lady Waring, which were almost complete, were destroyed by fire. The stalls were re-made and the carvings are a testimony to the skill of the woodcarver Mr. H. G. Ratcliff. The

# 1916

*On June 5th Lord Kitchener (1850/1916), who created a 'new army' when he organised the largest voluntary army ever seen in Britain, died when HMS Hampshire was sunk by a German mine.*

*Lt Col. Edward Henry Trotter, DSO, of the Grenadier Guards.*

inscription at the base of the stalls reads; 'In Loving Memory of Lord Waring's parents Samuel James Waring and Sarah his wife and of Lord and Lady Waring's only son Samuel Arthur Bamford Waring. A.D. 1924'. John Waring, who came to Liverpool in 1835 from Belfast, was responsible for the merging with Gillow & Co in 1897 to become Waring & Gillow.

A Cross for the Holy Table, in memory of Alfred Turner, was presented to the Cathedral by his daughter Maria Christina Noble.

Work began on the construction of the organ at the Great George Street works of Henry Willis and Sons Ltd. The specification was drawn up by Dr. Walter Henry Goss-Custard and Walter Ridley, nephew of the donor Mrs. Barrow.

The Stained Glass Committee accepted Messrs. Morris & Co's estimate for the cost of installing four large windows in the Chapter House. Until his death the company operated under the direction of William Morris (1834/1896) who played a prominent part in the arts and craft movement of the 19th Century. The firm continued under his successor John Henry Dearle (1859/1932) the stained glass designer.

Burlison and Grylls producers of stained glass windows commenced work on the Ambulatory windows.

## 1916

Some of the stained glass of the Lady Chapel windows was placed in position.

The Executive Committee accepted the proposal from the Captain Smith Memorial Committee that a window should be installed in the North Choir aisle annexe (now the Chapel of the Holy Spirit) in memory of Captain Edward John Smith, of the RMS *Titanic,* which sank on April 15th 1912. The committee agreed that the window should include figures that reflected Captain Smith's life as a seafarer and a traveller. Portrayed are; St. Christopher, crossing a river holding a child, St Nicholas, patron saint of sailors and holding a ship, St. Cuthbert, a traveller and St Chad of Lichfield, the Diocese in which he was born. Captain Smith came to Liverpool as an apprentice in 1867 and lived at various addresses in the Diocese. He joined the White Star Line in 1880 and was given his first command in 1887. In the same year he married Sarah Eleanor Pennington (1861/1931) at St. Oswald's Church, Winnick, near Warrington. They had one daughter Helen Melville Smith (1898/1973). A bronze statue of Captain Smith, unveiled in 1914, is situated close to Lichfield Cathedral.

Captain David Radcliffe (1894/1916) of the 24th Battalion the Royal Fusiliers, the only son of Mr. Frederick M. Radcliffe, Chairman of the Executive

Committee, and Mrs.Margaret Radcliffe, was killed on active service in France on March 18th. He is remembered with honour at Bully-Grenay communal cemetery, France. The North window, in the North West transept, entitled, *The Church in England,* is dedicated to him and his grandfather Sir David Radcliffe (1834/1907). In the following year Frederick Radcliffe's son in law Lt-Col, Alfred G. Horsfall (1876/1917) of the 2nd Battalion Duke of Wellington's Regiment died on October 9th and is buried at Bard Cottage cemetery, Belgium. He was the husband of Phyllis Radcliffe.

Lt. Montague Forwood Ainslie, son of Canon Richard Montague Ainslie and grandson of Sir William Forwood, died at Ypres on April 17th. Canon Ainslie, Vicar of All Saints, Childwall, was Chaplain of the 5th Battalion, The Kings (Liverpool) Regiment, and a member of the Executive Committee. A window in memory of Lt. Ainslie is to be found at All Saints Church, the King's Regiment badge is depicted at the bottom right hand corner of the window.

On June 5th Lord Kitchener (1850/1916), who created a 'new army' when he organised the largest voluntary army ever seen in Britain, died when HMS *Hampshire* was sunk by a German mine. He was an Honorary Freeman of the city and his name is recorded in the Cathedral's 'Roll of Honour'. Bishop Chavasse attended a service in his memory at St Nicholas Church, Liverpool. Lord Kitchener's Memorial Service was held in St Paul's, London.

Lt-Col, Edward Henry Trotter, D.S.O. (1872/1916) of the Grenadier Guards, who commanded the 18th Battalion, The Kings (Liverpool) Regiment, was killed on July 8th on the Somme. Lt-Col, Trotter became the commanding officer of the 18th Kings shortly after the Battalion was formed by the 17th Earl of Derby on August 29th 1914. As a result of Trotter's emphasis on physical fitness the 18th's prowess in the Inter-Battalion competitions earned them the soubriquet 'Trotter's Greyhounds'. The West clerestory window in the War Memorial Chapel is to his memory.

In August the Executive Committee agreed to set apart a definite portion of the Cathedral as a Memorial to all soldiers and sailors who fell in the war. Archdeacon Spooner and Chancellor Dowdall undertook to contact those interested in the project.

Lt. Norman Mather of the Kings Liverpool Regiment died on the Somme on August 9th. He was the son of Alderman Arthur S. Mather, a member of the Executive Committee. Alderman Mather was responsible for the 'Roll of Honour', which was initially displayed in the window of a ground floor office in Exchange Flags. The 'Roll of Honour', which is now preserved in the memorial hall within Liverpool Town Hall, was unveiled in 1921 by Edward, the Prince of Wales.

# 1917

*The death occurred of the Tranmere born ship owner James Hughes Welsford (1864/1917). In his will he left £700,000 to be divided equally between the Liverpool Shipowners Benevolent Society and the Cathedral Building Fund.*

*Bust of Captain Noel Godfrey Chavasse, carved by Mr Terry McDonald.*

Photo: © Gerry Simons

Photo: © Geoff Shipley

*Thomas Rigby public house sign, Dale Street, Liverpool.*

The Victoria Cross was awarded to Captain Noel Godfrey Chavasse the son of Bishop and Mrs Chavasse. Bishop Chavasse wrote to his son, 'You have been known so far as the son of the Bishop of Liverpool; I shall be known henceforth as the father of Captain Chavasse'.

The Revd George Hardwicke Spooner succeeded the Revd Thomas Madden as Archdeacon of Liverpool. His son Reginald Spooner (1880/1961) played cricket for Lancashire and made ten test match appearances for England in the years between 1905 and 1912. In 1912 he scored a century at Lords against South Africa.

The Revd George Howson was installed Archdeacon of Warrington.

It was felt that it was inappropriate that the White Star illustrated in the 'House' flag of the *White Star* Shipping Line should appear in the *Te Deum* Window. Accordingly, it was removed.

The architect was asked to have holes drilled in the vaults over the principal windows in the Choir so that cradles could be suspended for window cleaners.

Canon Harold E Bilborough (1867/1950), Rector of Liverpool, who helped lay the foundations of the Cathedral's musical and liturgical tradition, was consecrated Suffragan Bishop of Dover. In 1927 he was translated to Newcastle, where he served until 1941. The Cathedral frontal cupboards were a gift of Bishop Bilborough.

The death occurred of the organist and director of the choir Mr. Frederick Hampton Burstall (1851/1916) who organised the massed choirs at the laying of the Foundation Stone in 1904.

The Ambulatory windows, designed by Burlinson and Grylls at a cost of £800, were installed. The windows, which depict the national saints of England, Scotland, Ireland and Wales, were the gift of Louisa Emily Ashton Rigby in memory of her father Alderman Thomas Ashton Rigby (1816/1886). He was a wine and spirits merchant who owned a number of public houses in Liverpool, one of them being the well known *Rigby's* in Dale Street which he purchased in 1852. He lived with his family at 'Oakfield House' in Roby village He is buried in St Bartholomew's Churchyard, Roby.

Our Lady & St. Nicholas, originally a Chapel of Ease of Walton Parish Church, became the Parish Church of Liverpool.

## 1917

2nd Lt. Ralph Royds Brocklebank of the Welsh Fusiliers died in France on May 16th. He was the son of Ralph E.Royds Brocklebank, a member of the Executive Committee.

On July 3rd near Ypres, Aidan Chavasse of the 17th King's Liverpool Rifles L.R, was fatally wounded.

At Wieltje, Captain Noel Godfrey Chavasse (1884/1917) was fatally wounded and died at Brandhock, Belgian Hospital on August 4th. A bust of Capt. Chavasse, with the inscription 'A gallant and devoted officer', by the sculptor Mr. Terry McDonald, may be seen in the War Memorial Chapel.

On August 29th a Memorial Service was held at St. Nicholas, the Parish Church of Liverpool, for Noel Chavasse and for those of the Liverpool Scottish who lost their lives at Passchendaele. The address was given by Canon J. B. Lancelot, who later wrote Bishop Chavasse's biography.

At Liverpool Town Hall on October 5th a general appeal was launched by Sir John Utting, the Lord Mayor of Liverpool, to provide, as a Memorial for Sailors and Soldiers who fell in the First World War, 'a Transept in the Cathedral to be specially set apart for that purpose'.

Lt. Arthur Walter Stone R.N.V.R, son of Executive member Mr. John Stone, died in France in October. His name is recorded on the War Memorial in St Peter's Church, Heswall.

Captain Robert Elceum Horsfall of the King's Liverpool Regiment died in France on November 20th. He was the son of H. Douglas Horsfall who was a member of the Executive Committee from 1901 to 1905. The chancel screen at St Faiths, Crosby, was dedicated to Robert Horsfall's memory in 1921. The screen was designed by Giles Gilbert Scott.

On December 28th the Liverpool pilot boat *Alfred. H. Read* was struck by a German mine off the 'Liverpool Bar'. Nineteen Mersey pilots and twenty other ratings lost their lives. Their names are recorded in the Cathedral 'Roll of Honour'.

Dr. Walter Henry Goss-Custard succeeded Mr. Burstall as Cathedral organist.

The death occurred of the Tranmere born ship owner James Hughes Welsford (1864/1917). In his will he left £700,000 to be divided equally between the Liverpool Shipowners Benevolent Society and the Cathedral Building Fund. It was agreed that the porch on the North side of the Cathedral be named the Welsford Porch' to commemorate the magnificent bequest of the late Mr. J.H. Welsford to the Cathedral Building Fund'. In 1920 the family also contributed £5,000 to the War Memorial Transept Committee in memory of 2nd Lt, George Keith Welsford (1891/1916) of the

# 1918

*At 11am on November 11th the armistice between the Allies and Germany was signed, bringing to an end the First World War.*

Royal Flying Corps, son of James H. and Ethel Welsford, who was killed on active service on October 20th 1916. He is buried in Arras Flying Services Memorial, Pas de Calais, France. His name is also recorded on the Lychgate Memorial at St Mary of Antioch, Ivy Heath.

The continuing impact of the war, which led to a shortage of male clergy, witnessed the licensing of women as Lay Readers. They organised missions and in some instances ran church organisations. They were known as Bishops' Messengers.

A report in the *Scripture Reader* indicated that there were cases of financial distress among the workmen on the Cathedral site. Bishop Chavasse instructed the Clerk of Works to report to him on the matter. As a result one hundred pounds was placed at the Bishop's disposal to meet individual cases of hardship.

The architect put forward his proposals for the War Memorial Transept. The plans included a bronze grill to divide the Memorial Chapel from the rest of the Cathedral.

## 1918

On February 6th, the Representation of the People Act, giving the vote to women (aged over 30) for the first time, received the Royal Assent.

The death occurred of Mr. Herbert Plant Harrison (1869/1918). A corn merchant, he was one of the Honorary Treasurers and an original member of the Executive Committee. Windows to his memory are to be found in The Chapel of the Holy Spirit and the

*Musicians'* window in the Third Bay of the Nave. His son Colonel James M. Harrison (1913/1979) served on the Executive Committee for 32 years and was Chairman of the Committee from 1961. Colonel Harrison's ashes and those of his wife Anne lie in the North Choir aisle immediately below his memorial, which is incised into the North wall. His son Richard and his daughters Clare and Christina donated a painting entitled *'Crucifixion'*, in memory of their parents James and Anne. The painting hangs on the West wall of the Ambulatory.

Lt. William Gladstone, the son of the Rev Stephen Gladstone a member of the Executive Committee, was killed in action on September 27th. He was the grandson of William Ewart Gladstone who served as Prime Minister four separate times; 1868/1874, 1880/1895, 1886 and 1892/1894.

At 11am on November 11th the armistice between the Allies and Germany was signed, bringing to an end the First World War. More than a third of committee members suffered bereavement during the First World War; nine lost sons, one a grandson, and one a son-in-law. Throughout the war Bishop Chavasse, despite his own grief at the death of two sons, was able to bring comfort through his pastoral care to those in the Diocese who also suffered the loss of their loved ones.

The Revd Martin Linton-Smith (1869/1950), formerly Vicar of St Nicholas, Blundellsands and Rector of Winwick was consecrated, in the Lady Chapel, the first Suffragan Bishop of Warrington. In 1920 he was appointed Bishop of Hereford and in 1930 Bishop of Rochester where, in 1940, he was succeeded by the Revd Christopher Chavasse.

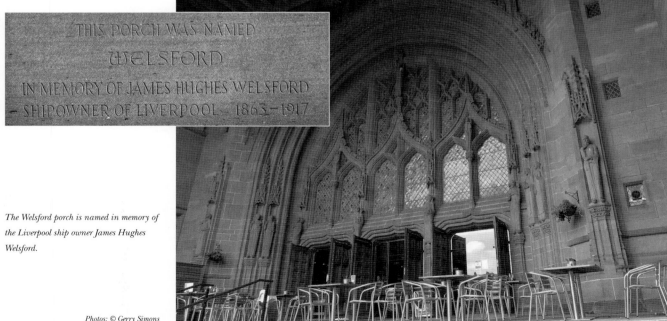

*The Welsford porch is named in memory of the Liverpool ship owner James Hughes Welsford.*

Photos: © Gerry Simons

# 1920

*Mr. Walter Gilbert (1871/1946), of the Bromsgrove Guild, was appointed to execute the sculpture of the Reredos at a total cost of £4,300.*

*Detail of bronze upright of the communion rail. Carving by Louis Weingartner representing the 6th Commandment; 'Thou shalt do no murder'.*

Photos: © Gerry Simons

*The Reredos, which took over four years to construct, is 65ft high and 48ft wide. The Reredos was the gift of Mrs. Agnes Wood in memory of her husband James Mark Wood, the Liverpool shipping owner.*

## 1919

The death occurred of Mr. Arthur Earle (1838/1919) an original member of the Executive Committee. The Old Testament window above the Welsford porch is dedicated to his memory and that of his wife Ida Euphemia's (1843/1903) memory. As one of the first officers of the committee his portrait appears in the *Laymen's* window in the South Nave aisle.

A memorial tablet was placed temporarily in the vestry of the Lady Chapel to Bishop Ryle. (Later superseded by the recumbent effigy of the Bishop in the South Choir aisle).

Mr. Hurlbutt's gift of £100 was allocated for the provision of a statue of Simeon on the left jamb of the St Matthew window as a memorial to his parents. Mr. Hurlbutt's request for an inscription was declined.  On the right jamb is a statue of St Anna. Statues on the jambs of the other Choir windows are; St Luke window- Aaron (left) and Elijah (right); St John Window- St James (left) and Cleopas (right); St Mark window-Nicodemus (left) and Jacob (right). The stone carvings beneath the St Matthew window are emblems of the Creation, beneath the St Luke window, emblems of the Passion, beneath the St John window, emblems of the Resurrection and beneath the St Mark window emblems of Baptism.

Representatives of the seven Boroughs of the Diocese, plus the Manor of Prescot accepted Sir William Forwood's scheme for the stained glass windows in the War Memorial Chapel to contain the arms of the boroughs. They are in the West Clerestory window; Liverpool, Warrington, St Helens and  Bootle. In the East clerestory window; Southport, Widnes, The

Manor of Prescot and  Wigan.

The North window of the War Memorial Chapel, *Sacrifice/Risen Life,* was donated by the Liverpool and District War Memorial Committee. The committee also met part of the cost of the Memorial Transept.

## 1920

Mr. Walter Gilbert (1871/1946), of the Bromsgrove Guild, was appointed to execute the sculpture of the Reredos at a total cost of £4,300.  To meet Giles Gilbert Scott's wish, that the focal point of the Cathedral should not be treated as a detached feature, the Reredos is structurally part of the East wall. The Reredos, which took over four years to construct, is 65ft high and 48ft wide. The principal sculptors were Walter Gilbert and Louis Weingartner of the Bromsgrove Guild.  The panels were cut by Arthur Turner of H.H. Martyn & Son of Cheltenham. The metal work was cast in their foundry.  The stone carvers were Messrs; M. Hoyle, J. Philips, W. Meadows, H.G. Radcliffe and E. Steel. G. Tosi of London did the gilding and decoration. The architect, for a tone effect, used a lighter Wooler stone from Northumberland rather than the local Woolton stone of the general structure.

The bronze communion rails were  donated by Mr. Thomas Taylor Wainwright in memory of Miss Lucy Wainwright. Each upright, cast in bronze at Martyn's foundry, is that of a woman in medieval dress and portrayed to reflect one of the ten commandments. The figures are the work of Louis Weingartner.  The oak communion rails were donated by the Queen Alexandra's Nurses' Fund. The Queen Alexandra's Imperial Nursing Service was established in 1902.

# 1921

*Construction of the Cathedral was back to normal for the first time since the end of the First World War.*

*Miss Adelaide Watt (1857/1921) of Speke Hall donated £1250 for the Bishop's Throne in memory of Richard Watt of Oakhill, ' a citizen' of Liverpool 1724-1796.*

The first President of the Service was Her Majesty Queen Alexandra.

At a ceremony in St George's Hall, to commemorate Bishop Chavasse's fiftieth year in the ministry, the Free Churches of Liverpool presented him with a car.

Negotiations for the sale of the site of St. Peter's Church to Harrods broke down.

The engineering company G. N. Haden & Sons Ltd of Liverpool were appointed to install a system of heating by means of a warm floor. Mr. George Nelson Haden's portrait appears in the *Laymen's* window. Featured alongside his portrait is a detail of the original central heating system which used hot air in ducts below the floor.

The Revd Edwin H. Kempson (1862/1931) was consecrated the second Suffragan Bishop of Warrington. From 1912 to 1920 he was Canon Residentiary at Newcastle Cathedral.

## 1921

In March King George V and Queen Mary visited the Cathedral site after attending a service conducted by Bishop Chavasse in the Lady Chapel. During the visit the King signed the prefatory page of the 'Roll of Honour'.

On the death of Mr. A. Green, Mr. Owen Pittaway, who had been employed on the site from 1906, was appointed Clerk of Works. Mr. Green's portrait, based on a photograph of him at the laying of the foundation stone in 1904, appears in the *Laymen's* window.

Construction of the Cathedral was back to normal for the first time since the end of the First World War.

Miss Adelaide Watt (1857/1921) of Speke Hall donated £1250 for the Bishop's Throne in memory of Richard Watt of Oakhill, ' a citizen' of Liverpool 1724-1796. On the ends of the desk are two sculptured figures of bishops by the sculptor Patrick Honan. On the East side St Denis, the Patron Saint of France and on the West side St Hubert who was Bishop of Leige, Belgium. Both countries were our allies in the First World War when the Bishop's Throne was in the course of construction.

In 1878 Adelaide Watt laid the foundation stone of All Saints Church, Speke, which was built in memory of her father Richard Watt who died in 1865. There is also a monument to Richard at Standish Church.

## 1922

Sir Alexander Hargeaves Brown (1844/1922), who donated the Lady Chapel window which depicts *Queen Margaret of Scotland* and *Queen Bertha of England*, died on March 12th. He was the grandson of Sir William Brown (1784/1864) merchant and banker who in 1860 erected, at his own expense, the Free Public Library and Museum in Liverpool.

In the New Year Honours List Frederick Radcliffe, Chairman of the Executive Committee, was knighted.

The site of St Peter's Church in Church Street was sold to Liverpool Corporation. Under the Act of 1902 the finance from the sale was allocated to the endowment of the Dean and Chapter. Some of the church furniture and fittings were relocated to other churches in the Diocese. A notable example being the placing of the carved reredos in St Cuthbert's Church, North Meols, Southport.

The Stained Glass Committee decided that in the case of the Woodward window, situated on the Chapter House staircase and not in the body of the Cathedral, to waive the rule 'that only a name and a date should appear in a window'. The window was the gift of Harvey Cecil Woodward of 'Northway House', Seaforth. He was a Liverpool corn merchant and a member of the Executive Committee. The window, which was designed and executed by the firm C.E.Kempe & Co, illustrates Biblical scenes of the story of corn and is in memory of four generations of the Woodward family.

Mrs. Mary Ann Temple, in memory of her husband Mr. John Temple (1839 /1922), presented twelve stalls surrounding the Bishop's seat. Mr. Temple was Managing Director and Chairman of Warrington Wire Rope Works. As an engineer he worked for the Atlantic Telegraphic Company and sailed on the *Great Eastern* when the second Atlantic cable was laid. His name is inscribed at the base of the stalls.

The stalls facing the Bishop's seat were presented as special gifts; twelve of them in memory of Harriet Newman and Katherine Ashe, ten of them by the Rural Deaneries of the Diocese. The names of the Deaneries inscribed on the brass plaques and fixed to the inside of the stalls are; Childwall, Liverpool South, Prescott, Toxteth, West Derby, Winnick, Wigan, Ormskirk, Walton and North Meols. Alderman A.S. Mather, Anne Caton, the Revd Leonard Rich, and Lilian Mary Wallace also have their names inscribed on brass plates.

The death occurred of Mr. Ralph Hindle-Baker, Warden of the Lady Chapel.

The Executive Committee decided that there should be no inscriptions in the War Memorial Transept in memory of individuals or of particular 'Units' of the Forces. Every part was to be in memory of those in the

# 1924

*On Wednesday September 17th the first administration of Holy Baptism in the Cathedral took place when the Revd F. W. Dwelly baptised Ursula Mary Brown.*

*Revd F. W. Dwelly*

*Bishop David succeeded Bishop Chavasse as acting Dean, they can be seen on this postcard commemorating the opening of Liverpool Cathedral in 1924.*

Diocese and local 'Units' who gave their lives in the First World War.

The architect's recommendation that no memorials should be permitted in any part of the Cathedral, in the form of metal or stone tablets affixed to the walls, was also accepted.

## 1923

On June 30th in a letter addressed to his Archdeacons, the Revd G. Hardwicke Spooner and the Revd George J. Howson, Bishop Chavasse announced to the Diocese his resignation of the Bishopric of Liverpool.

On September 24, in Liverpool Town Hall, Bishop Chavasse was presented with gifts comprising an illuminated address, a silver tea and coffee service and a cheque for £3807.

To commemorate his episcopate, the Arms of the Diocese, quartering Chavasse, were carved in front of the Bishop's Throne. He gave his farewell Blessing to the City from outside the Cathedral on the site that is known as 'The Founders' Plot'.

The installation of the Cathedral organ commenced on September 8th and part of the organ was used at the Consecration of the Cathedral .

On October 19th Dr. Albert Augustus David (1867-1950), who was consecrated Bishop in Westminster Abbey by Archbishop Davidson of Canterbury in 1921, was enthroned the 3rd Bishop of Liverpool at York Minster by Archbishop Lang of York. Bishop David served as Bishop of Edmundsbury and Ipswich from 1921 to 1923.

Bishop David succeeded Bishop Chavasse as acting Dean. Two Residentiary Canons were appointed.

The Stained Glass Committee approved the cartoon for the panel showing the death of Horatio Nelson

(1758/1805) in the War Memorial window, subject to amending the fact that he was depicted with three legs! Nelson was excluded, on moral grounds, from the *Te Deum* window but included in the War Memorial window on the grounds that 'he was portrayed as the instrument of Providence in a great national deliverance, not as typical of Christian virtue'.

## 1924

On January 22nd Ramsay MacDonald (1866/1937) became the first Labour Party Prime Minister. Throughout the year Liverpool witnessed many trade union disputes involving rail workers, dockers, bricklayers and masons.

On February 18th, a Protestant demonstration held in the Picton Hall, Liverpool, condemned the alleged ritualistic innovations in the Cathedral.

Liverpool's first local radio station (Radio 6LV) went on the air from a relay station located above the Edinburgh cafe in Lord Street, on June 11th. It was opened by the Lord Mayor of Liverpool, Alderman Thomas Dowd, from the Philharmonic Hall.

On Friday July 18th on the eve of the Consecration of the Cathedral a solemn night of unceasing prayer was held, on behalf of the Cathedral, the City, the Diocese, and the Church throughout the world. On the same evening the architect Giles Gilbert Scott was knighted at Knowsley Hall.

On Saturday July 19th the Consecration of the Cathedral, in the presence of H. M. King George V and H. M. Queen Mary, took place. The historic occasion is depicted in the *Church in England* window. For twelve year old chorister Robert Boye it was an occasion he would never forget as he sang solo. At 11am on Sunday July 20th The War Memorial Transept and Cenotaph were dedicated in the presence of H.M. King George V and H.M. Queen Mary.

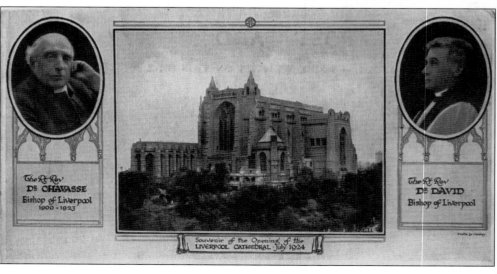

# 1925

*On January 17th the Memorial to the 55th West Lancashire Division, situated in the Derby transept, was dedicated by Bishop David.*

*The Memorial to the 55th West Lancashire Division, situated in the Derby transept, was dedicated by Bishop David. Designed by Sir Giles the sculptured group, modelled by Gilbert and Weingartner, was cut by Mr W. Meadows. The sculpture, which took six years to carve, depicts Marcel the 'Angel of Light' holding a crown above a kneeling soldier.*

On Monday July 21st the Chapter House, the gift of the Freemasons of West Lancashire, was dedicated by Bishop David in memory of the first two Earls of Lathom, and also of those Masonic brethren who had lost their lives in the First World War.

On Friday July 25th the installation of Bishop David took place. At the Service Lord Derby cut the first sod for the erection of the Central Space and the Western Transepts.

On Sunday July 27th a Thanksgiving Service brought to a close the consecration ceremonies.

In July a temporary refectory was erected at the West end of the site. The entrance was from St James' Road, up a flight of steps facing Mornington Terrace.

On Wednesday September 17th the first administration of Holy Baptism in the Cathedral took place when the Revd F. W. Dwelly baptised Ursula Mary Brown.

On Sunday September 28th the first ordinations were held in the Cathedral. R.H. Howat, G.M. Maudsley, F.A. Miller, W. Shuttleworth, R.B. White were ordained priest. J.A.J. Atkinson, A. Dixon, G.G. Elliot were ordained deacon.

On Wednesday October 1st the first confirmations at the Cathedral took place. There were 34 confirmation candidates.

On Wednesday October 8th Simon Arthur Cotton (1924/2003), the son of Colonel Vere E. Cotton, was baptised. It was the first Holy Baptism in the Cathedral administered by Bishop David.

On October 17th Edgar Francis James Chavasse (1924/2007) was baptised in the Cathedral by his grandfather Bishop Chavasse. His book *Chavasse Family History* 1669/2006 was published in 2007.

On October 20th William Arthur Thompson was baptised by the Archdeacon of Warrington Canon G.T. Howson.

The number of Residentiary Canons was increased to four and later to five.

The first official handbook, entitled *The Liverpool Cathedral,* by Vere E. Cotton, was published.

The Cathedral bookstall was opened. It was managed by Mr. Frederick Bulpitt.

Alderman Thomas Dowd J. P., the Lord Mayor of Liverpool presented a chair and faldstool for the use of the Lord Mayor. The chair was carved by H. G. Ratcliffe of London.

The architect submitted a provisional design for the Central Tower (it was to be 308 feet above floor level, instead of 342 feet as originally proposed).

The Lady Chapel windows were cleaned.

Canon Charles Raven inaugurated the late Sunday evening service which took place at 8.30pm.

Mr. Henry Heywood Noble, Honorary Treasurer and Senior Warden, presented 'The Cross of Liverpool'. The cross which is of silver bears the inscription 'Liverpool Cathedral 1924'. Mrs. Noble presented the altar cross in memory of her father Alfred Turner.

## 1925

On January 17th the Memorial to the 55th West Lancashire Division, situated in the Derby transept, was dedicated by Bishop David. Designed by Sir Giles the sculptured group, modelled by Gilbert and Weingartner, was cut by Mr. W. Meadows. The sculpture, which took six years to carve, depicts *Marcel* the 'Angel of Light' holding a crown above a kneeling soldier. An interesting feature of the design is the corbels supporting the memorial, which recall the Mark I tanks first used on the Somme in 1916. Included is the Divisional sign and motto 'They win or die who wear the rose of Lancaster', a quotation from a poem by Lieutenant Leonard Wall, written shortly before his death in action while serving with the Division. Givenchy-les-le-Bassee, the French mining village where many of the 55th Division lost their lives was adopted by Liverpool City Council. A Memorial Hall, for orphans and aged inhabitants, dedicated to the 55th was opened in 1924 by Alderman Thomas Dowd, Lord Mayor of Liverpool. The hall was destroyed during the Second World War.

On February 2nd a plain stone font, placed in the South Choir annex, was dedicated by Bishop David. The temporary font was the gift of the Children's Fund.

At Evensong on Saturday May 2nd the Revd F.W. Dwelly was installed by the Bishop of Liverpool as Canon of Liverpool *Ceremoniarus.*

'Cathedral Builders' as a subsidiary organisation to the Building Fund was founded, the first organisation of its kind in the country. The idea of an organisation to encourage regular giving to the Building Fund was suggested by the success of the Friends of the Fitzwilliam Museum at Cambridge (which in turn was based on *Les Amies du Louvre*). The annual subscription to become a Member was £1.05p. Subscribers were able to pay weekly, monthly or quarterly. Many Parochial Church Councils enrolled as members of the Cathedral Builders. By 1928 £7500 had been raised for the Cathedral Building Fund.

# 1926

*On September 19th on the eve of his 80th birthday Bishop Chavasse preached for the first and only time in the Cathedral.*

*Messrs Penlington and Batty, the Liverpool watch and chronometer makers, presented a small clock for the Lectern (now the Pulpit).*

In May Simon Cotton, son of Colonel Vere E. Cotton, was enrolled as the first 'Cathedral Builder'. He was followed by many who spent a lifetime collecting money for Cathedral funds. Amongst them Miss Olga Vaux (1901/1983), the daughter of a prominent Liverpool fruit trader, and her mother Beatrice who became members in 1928. When Olga died in 1983 she bequeathed £440,000 to the Cathedral. A sandstone plaque was unveiled to her memory in 1985 and is sited adjacent to the staircase window of the Lady Chapel.

In July the architect's final design of the Tower and Central Space was accepted by the Executive Committee. The tower was to be 331 feet in height and it is said to be the tallest gothic tower ever built.

On Saturday July 24th the first annual 'Builders' Service was held.

In September *The Liverpool Cathedral Bulletin,* as a journal of 'Cathedral Builders' was published for the first time.

On December 28th the first 'Grant of Arms' to the Cathedral was made by the Kings of Arms.

Bishop David moved his residence to Bishop's Lodge, Park Avenue, Mossley Hill. He had previously resided at 9 Greenbank Drive, Sefton Park..

A small alms plate designed by the architect and executed by Mr. Bainbridge Reynolds was presented by Major George Alexander Stokes Nairn, in memory of his parents Emma and George Nairn.

Twenty four bronze offertory plates, designed by the architect and executed by Mr. Bainbridge Reynolds, were presented by Mrs. and Miss Sutton Timmis in memory of 2nd Lt. Richard Sutton Timmis (1896/1915). The baptistery window is also to his memory.

Messrs Penlington and Batty, the Liverpool watch and chronometer makers, presented a small clock for the Lectern (now the Pulpit).

A fourteenth century silver-gilt chalice, part of the collection of Mr. Edward Rae, was presented by his family to the Cathedral, in his memory.

A silver alms dish for use in the Lady Chapel was presented in memory of Mary Elizabeth Neilson, the eldest daughter of Joseph and Ann Langton, who died in 1892.

Loud speakers were installed throughout the building. At the instigation of Bishop David the Cross of St Andrew (the 'Saltire'), with the Greek signs for *Alpha* and *Omega,* was carved on the floor of the Central Space where he made those marks with his pastoral

staff at the time of the consecration. Each year on the nearest Sunday to the anniversary of the consecration of the Cathedral the youngest chorister retraces the marks

Sir Frederick Radcliffe, Chairman of the Executive Committee, was created K.C.V.O.

The gradine, of black marble and partially gilt, situated behind the Holy Table in the Choir was rebuilt.

The walls which prevented it being possible to view the Sanctuary from the Choir aisles, other than through the bronze gates, were pulled down and replaced by an open screen.

The photographers Stewart Bale, of 53 Lord Street, Liverpool, were appointed official photographers to the Executive Committee. The company took the photographs of the consecration of the Cathedral.

A meeting of the Liverpool Cathedral Choristers' Old Boys' Association was held. The first President was Bishop David.

Bishop David instituted a College of Cathedral Stewards.

# 1926

In April the Cathedrals Commission, established in 1924 to report on the constitution, resources and requirements of Cathedrals, visited the Cathedral and its report was published in July.

On June 28th the decision was made to proceed with the work of building the Western Transepts simultaneously with the construction of the Central Space.

On September 19th on the eve of his 80th birthday Bishop Chavasse preached for the first and only time in the Cathedral. So large was the congregation that many were unable to gain entrance to the Cathedral. After the service, from the 'Founders' Plot', he addressed the crowd waiting outside. In the evening, at his own suggestion, he then preached at the Parish Church of St Martin's-in-the- Field, situated in Silvester Street, off Vauxhall Road. The church, which was erected in 1828, suffered damage during the Second World War and was demolished in the 1950's.

On December 20th the Chapel of the Holy Spirit, a place of prayer and meditation, was dedicated by the Acting Dean, Bishop David, who gave the Chapel its name. The reredos, with an alabaster figure of Christ in solitary prayer on the mountain overlooking the sea of Galilee, is the work of the architectural sculptor William Drinkwater Gough (1861/1938). In 1929 Sir

# 1927

*On July 3rd Mrs. Edith Jane Chavasse (1851/1927) wife of Bishop Chavasse, died.*

*Mrs. Edith Jane Chavasse (1851/1927) wife of Bishop Chavasse*

Giles used the skill of William Gough at St Alphege's Church, Bath, which was the architect's first design in the Romanesque style. A shield and effigy of the architect carved by William Gough is on the capital of a pillar in the church. It is perhaps the only sculpture of Sir Giles.

The cost, to defray the alterations to the North Choir aisle annexe to accommodate the small devotional chapel, was met by Sir William Forwood. He also donated a silver chalice, a paten, an Altar cross and vases. The aumbry is in memory of Mr. Thomas Utley (1854/1927). Thomas established a foundry in Tuebrook, Liverpool in 1881. In 1908 the company manufactured the portholes, windows and ship bells for HMS *Titanic*. Thomas had a ticket to sail but did not embark on the voyage as his wife had a premonition that something 'bad' was going to happen and persuaded him not to go.

The Revd F. W. Dwelly, who had served at Emmanuel Church Southport from 1916, was appointed to the Executive Committee.

The Cathedral organ was completed and dedicated on Saturday October 18th. It was at this time the largest church organ in the world. Each year an 'Anniversary' commemoration recital is given on the nearest Saturday to the date of the dedication. In addition to being played high up on the North side of the Choir a moveable recital console, manufactured by David Wells, was donated by Victor Hudson in 1989. Further additions; in 1997, a *'Trompette Militaire'*, the gift of Dr. Alan Dronsfield was installed 120 feet up in the Corona Gallery and in 2007 the Central Organ on the South Central Space Gallery, in memory of Eleanor Wright, who was Cathedral music administrator from 1989 to 2005.

Bronze gates, designed by the architect and executed by the Bromsgrove Guild, were erected at the head of the 'Bishop's stairway'. The gate was the gift of Mrs. M.G. Rollo as were the oak doors situated between the aisle and the Lady Chapel.

A stone and bronze alms chest which was placed in the South Choir aisle was presented by Mr. J. F. Caroe, the Liverpool corn dealer.

The clergy stalls in the Chapter House were completed, together with the Dean's seat on the East side. Inscribed on the back of this seat is the inscription 'the Freemasons of the Province of Lancashire, Western Division, in memory of Right Worshipful Brother Louis Slade Winsloe, Provincial Grand Master, 1919-1921'.

The name of Thomas Henry Ismay (1836/1899) was inserted in the bottom left-hand corner of the *Te Deum* window, above is the family motto 'Be Mindful'.

A silver plated Mace (The Cross of Liverpool Mace), the work of Mr. Horace Minns and bearing the arms originally intended to be adopted by the Chapter was presented by Mr. and Mrs. Howard Walker.

An oak cantor's chair, designed by the architect, was presented by Miss Stewart daughter of Canon Alexander Stewart (1826/1916). The West Gallery window, which depicts the *Collect for the Festival of the Annunciation,* commemorates his 34 years of ministry as Rector of Liverpool. In 1880 when St. Peter's became the Pro-Cathedral he became President of Honorary Canons which formed a provisional Chapter. He also served as one of the Bishop's Chaplains. From 1880, whilst neither in title nor stipend, he performed the role of Dean of the Pro-Cathedral. For twenty years he had sole responsibility of the musical service, the cost of which he defrayed himself. The *Liverpool Courier* records that his aim was 'to uphold a pure and majestic service'. Mrs Sarah Jones, wife of the former Bishop of Liverpool the Rt Revd James Jones, is the great, great-granddaughter of Canon Stewart.

Two flags were placed in the South East Transept. One, a large Union Jack which was broken at the mast of Government House Jerusalem in 1917 on the entry of the first British High Commissioner, General Edmund Allenby (1861/1936). The other being the Red Ensign presented, as a tribute, to Lt. Douglas R. Kinnier (1858/1916), Captain of the PSNC Ship, *Ortega.* The unarmed ship rather than surrender out-distanced and out-navigated her pursuers the German cruisers *Leipzig* and *Dresden* in September 1914.

Work commenced on building one of the main piers of the Central Space.

## 1927

On July 3rd Mrs. Edith Jane Chavasse (1851/1927) wife of Bishop Chavasse, died. Archdeacon Howson gave the Address and her husband Francis read the sentences of committal as she was laid to rest in the 'Founders' Plot', following the funeral service.

Despite approval by the Church Assembly and the House of Lords, on December 15th the revised *Book of Common Prayer* was rejected by the House of Commons

A small oak Credence Table was presented by Mrs. Ainslie in memory of Canon Richard Ainslie, Vicar of All Saints, Childwall and Chaplain to the 5th Battalion King's Liverpool Regiment Territorial Force.

A Processional Cross, designed by the architect, was presented to the Cathedral by the Liverpool Cathedral Old Boys Association in memory of Frederick Hampton Burstall, Organist and Master of the Choristers from 1881 to 1915.

# 1928

*On March 11th Bishop Chavasse died. His funeral service was held in St Peter's Church, Oxford.*

*Chair for use by the Lady Mayoress.*

Three faldstools were presented by Alderman Arthur S. Mather, Sir Frederick Radcliffe and Sir Charles and Lady Morton respectively.

Mr. William Lewis presented a Welsh Lectionary Bible in memory of the Most Revd John Owen (1854/1926) Bishop of St David's from 1897 to 1926.

Sir William Forwood presented the Cross and Vases for the Chapel of the Holy Spirit.

A chair and faldstool for use of the Lady Mayoress was presented by Sir Frederick Bowring (1857/1936) Lord Mayor of Liverpool.

The stone shields in the spandrels of the turret doorway of the Chapter House were carved with the arms of Sir Arthur Stanley and Mr. John H. Burrell past Grandmasters of the Masonic Province of West Lancashire.

A silver verge, the work of Mr. R.S. Minns of Hampstead, was presented by Sir Max and Lady Muspratt on the occasion of their son Rudolph's wedding on September 22nd. This was the first solemnisation of matrimony in the Cathedral. Sir Max also presented two faldstools.

Miss Norris presented an oak alms chest which was placed with an oak notice board, the gift of Sir William Forwood, outside the Chapel of the Holy Spirit.

The Revd Herbert Gresford Jones (1870/1958) was consecrated the third Suffragan Bishop of Warrington. From 1896 to 1904 he was Vicar of St. Michael-in-the-Hamlet, Liverpool and from 1923 to 1927 he was Vicar of Pershore, Worcestershire. In 1933 he presented to the Cathedral a bishop's crozier in memory of his father William Jones (1834/1902). Bishop Jones' son, the Rt Revd Edward Michael Gresford Jones (1901/1982) was Bishop of St Albans from 1950 to 1970.

Mr. H. H. Noble (1861/1934) the Cathedral Treasurer, presented a stone and bronze alms chest. It is situated at the East end of the South Choir aisle and bears the inscription; *Donum Henrici Heywood Noble am hvivs ecclesiae cathedralis thesaurari mdccccxxvii.* Above the chest is a text from Psalm 96. He also presented the alms chest which is placed against the pier which contains the foundation stone. At Easter Mr. and Mrs. Heywood Noble also presented an oak Credence Table for use in the Sanctuary.

The refectory, originally erected in 1907 as a hall for the men working on the site, was pulled down. A new refectory was erected in the East Court of the Cathedral site.

The death occurred of Mr. William Miles Moss (1864/1927), the Liverpool ship owner. He served on the Cathedral's General Committee in 1908. The East clerestory window situated above the shop, and which depicts the arms of India, Newfoundland, Southern Rhodesia and Jamaica, was donated by his wife Mrs. E.M. Moss to his memory. In addition she made a gift of £20,000 to the Building Fund.

The Bishop's Building Campaign was launched at Liverpool Town Hall to meet the growing and changing Diocese. The initiative witnessed the building of St. Michael, Blundellsands, St. Andrew, Clubmoor, St. Luke, Eccleston, St. Luke, Orrell and St. Stephen, Wigan.

## 1928

On March 11th Bishop Chavasse died. His funeral service was held in St. Peter's Church, Oxford. His body was brought to the Cathedral, and rested in the chancel until interment in the 'Founder's Plot' on Saturday, March 17th. The Thanksgiving Service was conducted by Bishop David with Archbishop Lang of York and Archbishop Evans of Wales, in attendance.

At a sitting on June 14th parliament again rejected the revised *Book of Common Prayer* despite changes having been made to the rejected 1927 version.

In July at the annual 'Cathedral Builders' service Miss Bickersteth was succeeded by Miss Dorothy Watts as secretary. Miss Bickersteth was presented with an *Etching of the Cathedral* by A. Brewer.

In October Mr. John Cornelius Vaughan (1862/1928) who had worked at the Cathedral for 24 years was accidentally killed when he fell off a wall.

In December Archbishop Cosmo Lang of York was translated to Canterbury.

Five oak alms boxes, designed by Sir Giles Gilbert Scott, were presented to the Cathedral. The donors were Sir Frederick Bowring, Alderman Arthur Mather, Alderman M. H. Maxwell, Sir Thomas Royden and Mr. John Stone.

The foundations of the Great Central Space and Western Transepts were completed. Lady Houston gave £10,000 in memory of her husband Sir Robert Houston (1851/1926), the Liverpool ship owner and Conservative M.P. for West Toxteth. In 1880 he established his own company R.P. Houston & Co. The company shipped supplies to South Africa during the Boer War (1899/1902). He is also credited with being one of the prime movers in the building of the New Brighton Tower. The West clerestory window situated above the shop and which depicts the arms of Australia, South Africa, New Zealand and Canada, is to his memory.

# 1928

*Sir William Bower Forwood (1840/1928), who was Chairman of the Executive Committee from 1901 to 1913, died in Funchal Madeira. In 1901 he raised, in six weeks, over £168,000 (£14 million in 2014 terms) for the Building Fund.*

The death occurred of Mrs. Phoebe Powell of Knotty Ash who was an original member of the Cathedral Embroidery Association. Amongst her work was The Festal Frontal used in the Lady Chapel.

A bound and printed copy of the Bible and Apocrypha in fourteen volumes, published by the Grolier Society, were placed in a special bookcase near the Chapel of the Holy Spirit. The Bible was presented by Canon Thompson Elliot and the bookcase was one of the last gifts made to the Cathedral by Sir William Forwood.

Miss Margaret Beavan the first woman Lord Mayor of Liverpool, affectionately known as 'the little mother of Liverpool' presented to the Cathedral a *Prayer Book* given to her by the city on relinquishing office.

The death occurred, in his eighty sixth year, of Mr. John W. Brown (1842/1928) the stained glass artist who designed the original Lady Chapel windows, the *Te Deum* window and the Choir windows. During his career he worked for both William Morris, at Merton Abbey, and Powells (Whitefriars). From 1886 he worked as a freelance but remained Powells preferred designer for prestigious projects.

The Liverpool shipowner and senior partner of Rankin, Gilmour & Co, Mr. John Rankin (1845/1928) died at his family home St Michaels Mount, St Michael in the Hamlet, Liverpool. He financed numerous worthy causes and promoted, on behalf of the Liverpool Institute of Archaeology, the British archaeologist John Garstang's excavations in Egypt. He received the 'Freedom of the City' in 1922 when he was described as 'one of the greatest citizens Liverpool ever had'. His gift of £20,000 was devoted to the great South porch in memory of the Rankin family.

Sir William Bower Forwood (1840/1928), who was Chairman of the Executive Committee from 1901 to 1913, died in Funchal, Madeira. In 1901 he raised, in six weeks, over £168,000 (£14 million in 2014 terms) for the Building Fund. Bishop Chavasse referred to him as 'the father of the Cathedral'. After the death of his first wife Mary Eleanor Moss (1842/1896) he married Elizabeth Le Fleming of Rydall Hall, Cumbria. He is buried in the War Memorial Chapel, at Bowness-On-Windermere which he had constructed.

The Liverpool Cathedral Choristers' Old Boys' Association was incorporated under the Cathedral statutes and, at the suggestion of Canon F. W. Dwelly, adopted the name 'Liverpool Cathedral College of Ex-Choristers'.

An album, containing eighteen large photogravure views of the Cathedral from photographs by Stewart Bale Ltd of 53 Lord Street, Liverpool, was published by the Photocrom Company. The family firm specialised in commercial and industrial photography. The Bale collection was acquired in 1986 and is housed in the Maritime Library.

A new refectory, situated in the East court of the Cathedral, was opened to the public.

# 1929

Severe weather during February and early March prevented work on the Cathedral.

At the beginning of Evensong on May 5th the bronze

*The Cathedral circa 1934 by Stewart Bale Ltd of 53 Lord Street, Liverpool.*

# 1929

*During the annual Nurses' Service on May 29th, a Memorial, to the twenty Liverpool nurses who gave their lives in the First World War, was unveiled in the Lady Chapel by Lady Annie Cowdray.*

*Sister Gwen Ainsworth whose name appears on the Lady Chapel memorial to the nurses.*

recumbent effigy of Frederick 16th Earl of Derby, the first President of the Cathedral Committee, was unveiled. Sir Giles Gilbert Scott was responsible for the general design with the assistance of the sculptors Mr. Thomas Tyyrrell (1857/1929) and Mr. Wilson. Messrs Farmer & Brindley Ltd undertook the modelling of the figure and the bronze casting was carried out by Mr. A.B. Burton of Thames Ditton. Mr. Tyyrrell who assisted in the modelling of the recumbent effigy died two days after the unveiling of the memorial. During his years as Governor General of Canada (1889/1893) the 16th Earl founded the Stanley Cup for ice hockey. As a result the memorial has a particular resonance with Canadian visitors to the Cathedral.

During the annual Nurses' Service on May 29th, a Memorial, to the twenty Liverpool nurses who gave their lives in the First World War, was unveiled in the Lady Chapel by Lady Annie Cowdray. In 1918 Lady Cowdray established the 'Nations Fund for Nurses', a benevolent society for those nurses who suffered as a result of war. The twenty Liverpool names are carved below the memorial immediately above which is the text 'They counted not their lives unto the death' (Revelation 12 v 11.). The memorial of Nebrasina marble was designed by Sir Giles Gilbert Scott. The bas relief is the work of the Lancashire sculptor Mr. David Evans.

The piers of a huge crane collapsed during a gale on September 20th causing damage to the gravestones in the cemetery.

A Memorial Tablet to Sir William Forwood, the first Chairman of the Executive Committee, incised into the wall of the North Choir aisle was dedicated by Bishop David.

The death of Alderman Arthur S. Mather (1843/1929), was announced. He was the youngest son of John Philips Mather the founder of Christ Church, Bootle. He was Lord Mayor of Liverpool 1915-16 and a member of the Executive Committee. Mather Avenue, Liverpool is named after him. In his memory the Mather family defrayed the cost of a new doorway into the Bishop's vestry. The single word 'Mather' was inscribed on one of the wrought iron hinges. Alderman Mather also donated one of the clergy stalls opposite the Bishop's throne. The stall is identified by a named brass plate

For the first time since the consecration the stained glass windows were cleaned both inside and out. The old Chaplain's House, which stood on the very edge of the slope overlooking the cemetery, was demolished. The work was carried out by S. J. Dyer of Walker Street, Liverpool at a cost of £25.

As an experiment the roof galleries on the South side

were opened to visitors for a charge of one shilling (5 pence).

Canon Dwelly was appointed Vice-Dean of the Cathedral.

A reading desk for the photographic copy of the 'Roll Of Honour' was placed against the wall to the left of the cenotaph (today the sound box is situated there).

Due to ill-health Miss Watts resigned as secretary of the 'Cathedral Builders'. Miss Bickersteth once more took up the reins of secretary.

Dr. Francis Neilson presented the enamelled terracotta sculpture the *Kneeling Madonna* to the Cathedral. It is attributed to the School of Luca della Robbia and was therefore made in the late 15th or early 16th century in Florence. The terracotta *Christ Child* figure, set alongside the sculpture, is by the artist Don McKinlay and is in memory of the fourth Dean of Liverpool the Very Revd Derrick Walters (1932/2000) who was Dean from 1983 to 1999. Dean Walters name is engraved on the paving at the entrance to the Choir where his ashes rest.

Mr. Fred Bower (1872/1942) of Heswall, one of the first stonemasons to work on the Cathedral and author of *Rolling Stonemason,* revealed in the *Liverpool Echo* that on the evening before the laying of the Foundation Stone he had hidden a letter, wrapped between copies of the *Clarion* and the *Labour Leader,* in a cavity of the brickwork on which the stone was laid. Motivated by the sight of the surrounding slums and poverty the letter reveals his displeasure that, 'several top-hatted gentlemen came along and two or three of them placed half sovereigns between the joints of the brickwork and stood by while another layer of bricks securely locked up the coins'. Also placed in the cavity is a copy of the *Order of Service.*

An oak music desk and a new oak microphone stand, designed by the architect, was presented to the Cathedral by Mr. C. J. Allen, in memory of his wife.

# 1930

In January the death occurred of Canon Morley Stevenson (1851/1930). He was Principal of Elphins, Warrington, a boarding school for Clergy Daughters' from 1880 to 1883 and Principal of the Teachers' Training College, Warrington. He was a member of the Executive Committee from 1923 until 1927. He assisted the Revd F.W. Dwelly in the planning of the Consecration Service in 1924. His contemporaries said 'he endeared himself by his charming and saintly character'. The East clerestory window of the Baptistery was presented, to his memory, by his wife Mrs. Stevenson. The window depicts the arms of

# 1930

*Edward Carter Preston, the artist and medallist, received his first Cathedral commission to design the four figures to be placed on the mullions of the transept windows.*

*Sculpture by Edward Carter Preston. Figure of St. Paulinus, the first Bishop of York.*

Sydney, Gibraltar, Toronto and Sierra Leone

In February alterations were carried out to the platform on which the Holy Table stands. To allow for the addition of three extra steps the centre of the platform was brought forward towards the altar rail. The marble credence table on the right was converted into a sedile. Mr. H. Sutton Timmis met the cost of the alterations.

Mr. Patrick Honan, the sculptor who did a large amount of work at the Cathedral both as carver and modeller, died on March 25th at the age of 67 years.

On Sunday July 30th a Jubilee Service was held to commemorate the fiftieth year of the Liverpool Diocese. Similar services took place across the Diocese. The Rt Revd H. Gresford Jones presided over diocesan celebrations held in September. The *Liverpool Review* published a special 'Diocesan Jubilee Number' to celebrate the occasion.

*The Fiftieth Year: The Liverpool Diocese,* by Edward Carter Preston, which contains three full page wood-engravings and three decorations by Edward Carter Preston was published by J.A. Thompson & Co. Two hundred and fifty numbered copies were printed.

Bishops attending the Lambeth Conference were invited to a special service in the Cathedral. Archbishop Charles Longley (1794/1868), who convened the first conference in 1867, is depicted in the *Bishops'* window.

On November 11th at 11a.m the Liverpool Cenotaph, which stands on the plateau of St George's Hall and which is dedicated to the memory of those from Liverpool who died in the First World War, was unveiled by the 17th Earl of Derby. The Memorial Service was conducted by Bishop David. The sculpture is the work of Herbert Tyson Smith (1883/1972), whose work is also to be found in the Cathedral

Miss Lederer presented to the Cathedral an oil painting of Bishop Ryle.

Miss Mabel Tunstall was appointed secretary of 'Cathedral Builders'.

A crozier, in memory of Sir William B. Forwood, was presented by the Forwood family for the use of the Bishops of Liverpool when officiating in the Cathedral. The crozier of silver, which was used for the first time on Easter day, was designed by Sir Giles Gilbert Scott and executed by Mr. Bainbridge Reynolds.

The bound volume of the 'Roll of Honour', which contains the names of nearly 40,000 men from the Diocese of Liverpool who gave their lives in the First World War, was completed and placed in the

Cenotaph. It is the work of the heraldic artist Mr. George Scruby. He was assisted by his daughter Audrey (Mrs. Krohn) The binding was carried out by Messrs G. Sangorski and G. Sutcliffe of London.

A Donors Book similar in material to the 'Roll of Honour' was also designed by Mr. Scruby and bound by Mr. Sutcliffe.

Mrs. Herbert Leventon met the cost of providing a copy in the form of a photographic reproduction of the original 'Roll of Honour'. The photographic copy is in memory of 2nd Lt Raymond Sylvester Leventon, Pilot R.F.C. who died on November 5th 1917 aged 19 years. He lost his life when the plane, which he was flying over the sea, collapsed as a result of the breaking of a wing. His body was never found. His name appears upon a memorial stone in St James cemetery, Dover. Raymond was the eldest son of Mr. and Mrs. Herbert Leventon of Thornton Leigh Huyton. Mr. Leventon was chairman of the Liverpool newsroom.

A Reader's Desk (The Ambo) in memory of Dr. Richard Caton (1842/1926), Lord Mayor of Liverpool (1907/08) and a member of the Executive Committee from 1912 to 1926, was placed in the Cathedral by members of his family. Dr. Caton also donated a stall opposite the Bishop's throne. The brass plate reads,' In beloved memory of Anne Caton (nee Ivory) 23rd June 1912'.

An illuminated volume, the work of Mr. John Buchanan, recording the names and units of the nurses from Liverpool who gave their lives on service in the First World War was placed in a small oak lined recess at the side of the Nurses' Memorial in the Lady Chapel. The book was the gift of Miss Bramwell.

The heating system of the Cathedral was converted from coal to burn oil fuel.

Edward Carter Preston, the artist and medallist, received his first Cathedral commission to design the four figures to be placed on the mullions of the transept windows. (*St Barnabas* on the exterior mullion of the South Arm Western Transept, *St Paulinus* on the exterior mullion of the North West transept, *St Raphael* and *Tobias* on the interior mullion of the Baptistry window, and the Angel Ithuriel on the interior mullion of the *Church in England* window.

The term 'Cross Guild' began to be used to describe the former choristers.

A College of Interpreters was formed to welcome visitors and explain the building and its message. The diocesan clergy who took up the role were known as 'Priest Interpreters'.

Colonel Robert Ireland Blackburne (1850/1930), who

# 1931

*The first representation in stained glass of Liverpool Cathedral was the memorial window at Christ Church, Sefton Park, dedicated to Canon Robert Irving (1840/1922) where he was vicar for 45 years.*

*The Cross of Liverpool Mace donated by the Cross Guild.*

donated the Lady Chapel window which depicts *St Agatha* and *St Prisca*, died. He was a descendant of John Blackburne the ship owner and owner of the Liverpool Salt House dock. John Blackburne built Blackburne House situated in Hope Street which, from 1844 to 1984, was the Liverpool Institute High School for Girls.

## 1931

On May 18th The Board of Finance issued a 'Declaration of Trust' for the maintenance of the War Memorial Chapel. The Chapel was to be known, recognized and called the War Memorial Chapel in perpetuity.

On June 29th the Dean and Chapter were incorporated by an Order in Council. This was the first time since the reformation that such an order had been made.

At the British Legion Service on July 16th Major General Sir Fabian Ware (1869/1949), the founder of the Imperial War Graves Commission, presented to the Cathedral a wooden cross from the grave of an unknown soldier in Flanders.

The new Chapter received from the College of Heralds a grant of Arms. The heraldic description reads; *Argent A Patriarchal Cross throughout Gules* (a double armed cross in red on a silver ground). The seal of the Chapter, which was designed by Edward Carter Preston, represents the 'Risen Christ in glory rising over the arms of the Chapter'.

On July 26th the Memorial to Bishop Chavasse was unveiled by Sir Frederick Radcliffe at the afternoon service. The general design of the memorial is by Sir Giles Gilbert Scott. The carving of the memorial, which is of Derbyshire light fossil marble, was carried out by Mr. Peter Induni from Mr. David Evans' plaster model. The red sandstone background including the relief of the Cathedral was cut by the Liverpool stonemason Mr. Joseph Phillips.

On Sunday October 4th The Very Revd F.W. Dwelly was installed as the First Dean of Liverpool. At the service the address was given by the Poet Laureate John Masefield (1878/1969).

In October the Revd Christopher Chavasse preached at the Liverpool College Commemoration Service. The Revd Chavasse and his twin brother Noel were educated at the college.

In November the Degree of Doctor of Divinity was conferred upon Dean Dwelly.

Canon C.E. Raven was appointed Chancellor of the Cathedral

Canon William Elsley, Vicar of St Anne's, Stanley (1908/1934) and the first Chapter Clerk, presented a printed edition of *The Chapter Course of Praises*. At the request of Bishop David Canon Morley Stevenson and the Revd Dwelly prepared the *Course of Praises* which is drawn from the Psalms and Gospels. St Anne's Church, the gift of Mr Thomas Fenwick Harrison, was consecrated by Bishop Ryle on September 27th 1890.

Mr. Malcolm West was appointed as Cathedral Bursar.

Mr. Stanley Williams was appointed the Dean's Clerk.

The first representation in stained glass of Liverpool Cathedral was the memorial window at Christ Church, Sefton Park, dedicated to Canon Robert Irving (1840/1922) where he was vicar for 45 years. He also served as Hon. Secretary of the Liverpool Diocesan Board of Education.

A representation of the Cathedral in stained glass was unveiled at St. Nicholas's Church, Wallasey. The Church was erected by Mr. Fred Harrison and Sir Heath Harrison in memory of their parents James and Jane Harrison who founded the Harrison Shipping Line. The family were generous subscribers to the Cathedral Building Fund.

A Memorial Service for Miss Margaret Beavan (1877/1931), Lord Mayor of Liverpool 1927 to 1928, was held at the Cathedral. Miss Beavan was an active campaigner for the welfare of children and served on the Liverpool Child Welfare Association's Committee.

The Cathedral Cross Guild was inaugurated. One of the founder members of the guild was Mr. William J. Hunter (1909/1991) who became a Cathedral chorister in 1920. He served as President of the Cross Guild until 1983. In 1967 he was appointed to supervise the Cathedral book shop and act as information officer for visitors to the Cathedral. His ashes lie in the South Nave aisle where there is an inscribed memorial stone. In memory of him the Cross Guild presented to the Cathedral 'The Cross of Liverpool Mace', inscribed; 'by Fellow Members of his beloved Cross Guild'.

Mr. Lewis Charles Steinhoff (1889/1931) a French and English spindle moulder, who worked on the woodwork in the Lady Chapel, died.

Mr. John Joyce (1861/1931), a labourer on the Cathedral site for nearly thirty years died.

## 1932

On Saturday January 9th Thomas Aidan Chavasse, grandson of Bishop Chavasse, was baptised. Thomas's name was the first on the Cathedral's 'Roll of Welcome' to the Church of England.

# 1933

*The first burial within the Cathedral took place in January when the ashes of Sir Robert Jones (1857/1933), the orthopaedic surgeon, were laid to rest in the gallery of the South arm of the Eastern transept over the Derby Memorial.*

*Agnes Jones (1832/1868), the first lady superintendent of the workhouse hospital (1786/1860). This stained glass window is located in the Lady Chapel.*

On February 9th a 'Kinship with the Sea' Service was held. The service included a reading by John Masefield of his poem *Masque of Liverpool* and music for the *Psalms of the Sea.*

The Duke and Duchess of York (later King George VI and Queen Elizabeth) visited the Cathedral on June 21st.

A Thanksgiving Service was held on November 13th to commemorate the centenary of the birth of Agnes Jones (1832/1868), the first lady superintendent of the workhouse hospital and the inauguration of the first public washhouse by Kitty Wilkinson (1786/1860). Portraits of Agnes and Kitty appear in the staircase window.

Canon C.E. Raven was appointed to the *Regius* Professorship of Divinity at Cambridge.

Canon James S. Bezzant was appointed Canon Residentiary and Chancellor of the Cathedral.

The Cathedral Embroidery Association with its work completed was dissolved.

*The Liverpool Cathedral Bulletin* was adopted as the official chronicle of the Cathedral Committee.

The eighth edition of the official handbook, entitled *The Cathedral,* was published.

The inside of the dome of the Chapter House was lined with celotex acoustical slabs and the floor of the gallery with a sound absorbing material called Cabot Quilt.

Mr. H. Heywood Noble, Honorary Treasurer of the Executive Committee from 1914, resigned.
He was succeeded by Colonel A.C. Tod and Sir Charles Morton who acted as joint Honorary Treasurers.

An anonymous donor gifted to the Executive Committee the ownership of the 16th century Cantorist House, situated in the village of Childrey near Wantage, Berkshire. The property was sold in 1939 and the proceeds deposited in the Building Fund.

## 1933

The first burial within the Cathedral took place in January when the ashes of Sir Robert Jones (1857/1933), the orthopaedic surgeon, were laid to rest in the gallery of the South arm of the Eastern transept over the Derby Memorial. He was knighted in 1917 when he was described as 'the greatest orthopaedic surgeon in Britain'. In 1937 his ashes were placed behind his memorial stone in the South Choir aisle.

On March 21st Mr. N. Hannah, a joiner, died after falling from a scaffold on to the vault platform a distance of some 30 feet. This was the third fatality to occur in connection with the building.

On Saturday May 6th the Bishop Ryle memorial was dedicated. The recumbent effigy, of alabaster, was designed by Sir Giles Gilbert Scott and the figure was the first work of Edward Carter Preston to be erected in the Cathedral.

The death occurred of the Archdeacon of Liverpool the Revd George Hardwicke Spooner (1852/1933), who was a member of the Executive Committee from 1901 and Archdeacon of Liverpool from 1916.

The Revd George Howson was installed Archdeacon of Liverpool.

Mr. H. Sutton Timmis (1867/1933) resigned as Secretary to the Executive Committee. He was succeeded by Lt-Col. V.E. Cotton.

A Precentor's chest for the Chapter House, in memory of Ralph Hindle-Baker, Warden of the Lady Chapel, was presented to the Cathedral. Mr. Baker, who founded the Church Choir Association in 1899, organised the massed choir for the 'Foundation Stone Laying Service'.

He was the author of *The Organist and Choirmaster's Diary.* The diary provided all that was 'necessary to an organist and choirmaster for keeping a record of everything appertaining to his Church and choir in the handiest possible form'.

Mr. Croston, Secretary to the 'Cathedral Builders', resigned. He was succeeded by Miss Grace B. Scott.

The base of the Ryle memorial was altered, the architect substituting sandstone for the marble and remodelling the whole of the lower part of the memorial.

The death occurred of Mr. J. Greville Earle, a member of the Executive Committee for twenty one years. His father Mr. Arthur Earle was an original member of the committee.

Dean Dwelly's invitation to the Unitarian preacher Dr. Lawrence Pearsal Jacks (1860/1955) to preach in the Cathedral was met with considerable outrage and a rebuke from the Convocation of the Church of England.

The Executive Committee accepted Mrs. H. R. Hornby Lewis' offer of the rose window, *The Holy Trinity,* on the south side of the tower. as a memorial to her husband Arthur Hornby Lewis. J.P, a copper merchant and High Sheriff of Cheshire. His name is inscribed on the South wall of the under-tower to the west of the circular light and only visible from the Corona gallery.

# 1934

## 1934

*In March it was announced that Lord William Vestey and his brother Sir Edmund Vestey undertook to defray the cost of building the Central Tower in memory of their parents Samuel Vestey (1832/1902) and Hannah Vestey (1836/1884).*

*10th Anniversary medal given to the workmen who had been employed for 10 years or more on the building of the Cathedral.*

*Work commenced on the building of the Tower. This was Sir Giles Gilbert Scott's sixth design.*

The Cathedrals (Amendment) Measure, declared the Principal Chapter to be the consenting body for the purposes of the Cathedral Measure 1931. As a result the constitution and statutes of the Cathedral were revised.

Work commenced on the building of the Tower. This was Sir Giles Gilbert Scott's sixth design.

In March it was announced that Lord William Vestey and his brother Sir Edmund Vestey undertook to defray the cost of building the Central Tower in memory of their parents Samuel Vestey (1832/1902) and Hannah Vestey (1836/1884). William and Edmund established the Vestey empire in 1897. They were pioneers of refrigeration, opening a cold store in London in 1895.

Sir Max Muspratt (1872/1934), director of Imperial Chemical Industries Ltd, died on April 20th. His widow Lady Helena presented to the Cathedral a number of rare liturgical books which are now deposited at Hope University library.

On May 16th the death occurred of Sir Heath Harrison (1857/1934) a member of the Liverpool ship owning family. His gift of £25,00 to the Cathedral Building fund was only revealed after his death. A window to his memory is to be found in Portsmouth Cathedral, where he was also a generous benefactor.

In June Sir Frederick Morton Radcliffe, Chairman of the Executive Committee, resigned. Colonel Alan Cecil Tod (later Sir), succeeded him as Chairman.

The plans for a library were accepted and it was to be known as the Radcliffe Liturgical Library.

H.M. King George V and H. M. Queen Mary, who visited the Cathedral, assented to their statues being included in the sculpture surrounding the doorways leading from the Rankin Porch into the Central Space.

On July 14th to mark the 30th anniversary of the laying of the foundation stone two hundred staff of Messrs Morrison & Sons, employed on the building of the Cathedral, were entertained to dinner at Reece's restaurant. Parishes throughout the Diocese celebrated the 30th anniversary with special services and events.

To celebrate the 10th anniversary of the consecration of the Cathedral a special medal, designed by Edward Carter Preston, was struck. It was the gift of Sir Frederick Radcliffe to forty six workmen who had been employed for 10 years or more on the building of the Cathedral. The name of each recipient was engraved on the rim of the medal. Replicas of the medal were issued in 2004 to celebrate the centenary of the laying of the foundation stone.

To mark the opening on Wednesday July 18th, of the Mersey Tunnel a special service was held in the Cathedral on Sunday July 15th. The Service included the 'Lighting of the Seven Lamps' of Faith, Charity, Commerce, Vision, Progress, Remembrance and Youth.

On December 15th the Ecclesiastical Commission found that there was no prima facie case for instituting proceedings against Dean Dwelly of 'causing great scandal' by refusing to execute the Bishop's mandate to install the Revd Cyril Twitchett as

# 1936

*On Monday January 20th King George V died. A Memorial Service was held in the Cathedral. It was not possible to accommodate all those who wished to attend the service.*

*The K6 or 'Jubilee' telephone kiosk, designed by Sir Giles Gilbert Scott.*

Archdeacon of Liverpool and the Revd J. Barker as Archdeacon of Warrington.

Bishop David returned from his visit to Australia.

The architect's design for the floor under the Tower received approval. The materials used were the same as that used in the Choir flooring, namely; Hopton Wood and black fossil marbles with a limited amount of yellow sienna marble.

As a result of Lord Salisbury's gift the quarry at Woolton became the property of the Executive Committee. The quarry, which had been worked for more than three hundred years, had previously formed part of the Childwall estates of the Cecil family.

Mr. M. Louis Weingartner the Swiss born sculptor, whose work with Walter Gilbert in the Cathedral, included the Reredos, died in a road accident in Lucerne.

Mr. T. Pagan, who from 1931 had acted as the manager of the bookstall, died. The bookstall, which was in the hands of the Cathedral Development Committee, was handed over to the Dean and Chapter.

The Revd C.F. Twitchett resigned his Residentiary Canonry, a position he had held since 1931, on his appointment as Archdeacon of Liverpool. He was also general Diocesan Secretary and editor of the *Liverpool Diocesan Calendar.* His position of Residentiary Canon was taken by the Revd J.T. Mitchell.

## 1935

In August the steel work on the tower was completed.

Three caskets, containing the ashes of Lord Vestey's father, mother and sister, were built into the wall at the base of the tower to the right of the doorway leading to the Welsford Porch.

Mr. W. Bainbridge Reynolds, the wrought iron artist who executed much of the metal work in the Cathedral, died at the age of eighty years. He features in the *Laymen's* window and is depicted holding the silver gilt cross from the high altar. Further examples of his work are to be found at St Cuthbert's Church, Philbeach Gardens, London.

On the 250th anniversary of the 2nd Battalion of the King's Liverpool Regiment, the ceremony of the 'laying up' of the colours took place in the War Memorial Chapel.

Lt. Col. V.E. Cotton the Honorary Secretary of Cathedral Builders resigned. He was succeeded by Mr. H. D. Woodsend.

To celebrate King George V and Queen Mary's Silver Jubilee, services were held throughout the Diocese. Parish churches were encouraged to sing the hymn *I vow to Thee my Country* by Sir Cecil Spring-Rice (1859/1918) whose portrait is to be found in the Hymnologist's window. The celebrations also included the introduction of the K6 or 'Jubilee' telephone kiosk, designed by Sir Giles Gilbert Scott, one of which is to be found in the Cathedral by the tower lift. It was donated by British Telecom.

The death occurred of Mr. George Rollo (1852/1935) who served on the Executive Committee for twenty seven years. Mr. Rollo was Vicar's warden at St Mary's Church, Waterloo. He was a senior partner in the firm David Rollo & Sons, Fulton Engine Works, Liverpool.

## 1936

On Monday January 20th King George V died. A Memorial Service was held in the Cathedral. It was not possible to accommodate all those who wished to attend the service. At this time it was possible to seat 540 people facing East and 240 people in the Transepts. Memorial Services were held across the Diocese.

On September 27th to mark the closure of the Mortuary Chapel a short service was held. The Chapel described as 'being of pure Grecian Doric architecture', was designed by the architect John Foster (1787/1846).

Under the Liverpool Corporation Act of 1936, St James' Cemetery, which was opened in 1829, was closed for burials and the Corporation became responsible for its upkeep in place of the former Board of Trustees.

On December 5th King Edward VIII abdicated.

In a radio broadcast, on December 27th, Archbishop Lang of Canterbury launched an evangelistic campaign entitled 'Recall to Religion'.

The death occurred of Mr. John Stone, a colliery proprietor and member of the Executive Committee for twenty four years. His son Thomas was a member of the committee from 1921 until his death in 1963, his son Thomas jnr. also served on the committee. A unique record of three generations of service. The family lived at 'The Orchard', Huyton with Roby. The left lancet of the 'New Testament' window is in memory of John Stone (1842/1936) and his wife Isabella (1843/1933). The cost of the window was defrayed by Mr. Thomas Stone and his sister Mrs. Segraves.

# 1937

*The Coronation of King George VI took place on May 12th.*

*The font with the oak baldachino donated by Mrs. Helen Swift Neilson of Chicago.*

## 1937

On February 8th, at the age of 83 years, the death occurred of Mr. William Morrison head of the firm Messrs Morrison and Sons, Ltd, the contractors to the Cathedral. Mr Morrison features in the *Laymen's* window alongside a quarry-man.

The artist Mr. Thomas Raffles Davison (1854/1937) the architectural illustrator and journalist, who was the author of the drawings of the tower and the central space, died on May 5th.

The Coronation of King George VI took place on May 12th.

To mark 'Coronation Year' it was suggested that parents, 'in search of suitable birthday presents for their children, enter their sons and daughters on the roll of 'Cathedral Builders'.

On June 6th 2,000 people, representing Anglican and Non-Conformists, joined together in a unique service entitled 'The Empire Broadcast Service of Affirmation'.

In December the temporary wall was taken down and the Central Space was revealed.

Mr. James S. Rankin, son of the donor of the Rankin porch Mr. John Rankin, was elected to the Executive Committee.

Alake of Abeokuta and H.I.H. Prince Chichi, the brother of the Emperor of Japan, visited the Cathedral.

An album, entitled *Liverpool Cathedral,* a collection of photographic views of the Cathedral was published by Young & Sons Ltd of Liverpool.

A Memorial Stone to Sir Robert Jones, behind which rest his ashes, was unveiled in the South Choir aisle. The panel, which is of Hopton wood marble, shows the distinguished surgeon operating upon a child with a nurse in attendance. Incised above the scene is the family crest with the motto; *Gobaith Ysgavnha Lafur* (Hope Lightens Labour). The memorial was designed by Sir Giles Gilbert Scott and sculpted by Edward Carter Preston.

A temporary West wall which closed the Nave Arch was erected. Unlike its predecessor, situated between the Eastern Transept and the Under-Tower, it was of wood not brick.

The death occurred of the heraldic artist Mr. George Scruby (1868/1937). Mr Scruby inscribed the Cathedral's the Book of Remembrance.

The Lord Mayor of Liverpool Alderman Denton, as a mark of appreciation, invited the Clerk of Works and representatives of the various trades engaged on the work of building the Cathedral to lunch at the Town Hall.

Sir Benjamin Sands Johnson (1865/1937), who was managing director of Johnson Dyers, the cleaning firm and Chairman of the Diocesan Board of Finance, died. The right lancet of the New Testament window was donated by Lady Johnson and Mrs. R. Pyemont to his memory. The central lancet was given by B.B. Gardner in memory of Richard Cardwell Gardner, director of the wine and spirit company Gardner & Jackson. He was Mayor of Liverpool from 1862 to 1863 and Gardners Drive, Liverpool was named after him. The family resided at Newsham House, Tuebrook, which was later used as a lodging house for visiting judges.

Sir Giles Gilbert Scott was appointed architect to the King George V National Memorial.

The casts of the figures, designed by Edward Carter Preston, for the interior doorways on each side of the Central Space were displayed in the former Mortuary Chapel. The figures over the doorway leading to the Welsford Porch represent the theological or supernatural virtues of Faith, Charity (as primary, is over the central door) and Hope. The eight lower figures represent the 'Natural Virtues' with at the feet of each figure its anti-thetical vice. Over the doorways leading to the Rankin Porch are; in the centre Theology and on either side Philosophy and Natural Science. Below are figures representing the 'Liberal Arts and Sciences of Mankind'. The figures were sculpted by Mr. Reginald Yorke.

## 1938

'The laying up 'of the old colours of The Liverpool Scottish, formerly the 10th Battalion of the King's Regiment, took place in the Cathedral at a service held on Sunday May 22nd .

In June it was revealed that the anonymous donor of the oak baldachino, which surrounds the font, was Mrs. Helen Swift Neilson of Chicago. The oak font cover was the gift of Mr. Thomas Pegram, of Hoylake, in memory of his wife Mrs. Alice Mary Pegram.

On November 5th the death occurred of Mrs. Helen Johnston (1856/1938) wife of Mr. Edmund Johnston (1852/1934). Mr. and Mrs. Johnston defrayed the cost of the carvings on the entrance on the South side of the under-tower. A memorial to them is carved on the floor at the entrance of the Rankin porch.

Mears & Stainbank at Whitechapel, London commenced work to cast the ring of the Cathedral's thirteen bells. The firm which was founded in 1570, cast Big Ben, Great Tom of St Paul's and those of Bow Church.

# 1939

*At noon on September 3rd the Prime Minister Neville Chamberlain made his solemn announcement that the country was at war with Germany.*

*Hignett cigarette card.*

*Clearing high explosive bomb damage to the Rankin Porch*

Mr. S. Fawcett Hignett defrayed the cost of the West clerestory window of the Baptistry which depicts the arms of the Sees of Calcutta, Capetown, Auckland and Washington, in memory of his parents Mr. John Hignett (1830/1898) and Mrs. Sarah Anne Hignett (1839/1933). Mr. John Hignett was a Liverpool tobacco manufacturer. The family lived at Mere Lane, Walton, Liverpool.

## 1939

Their Royal Highnesses the Duke and Duchess of Kent visited the Cathedral on July 7th. The Duchess made a trip to the top of the tower. Amongst those presented to the Duke and Duchess was Mr. J. Miller, a mason who joined the Cathedral's workforce in 1907.

At noon on September 3rd the Prime Minister Neville Chamberlain made his solemn announcement that the country was at war with Germany. Government restriction on building works had an inevitable impact on the progress of the building. However, in view of the size of the windows the decision was taken not to protect them.

The death occurred on September 26th of Mrs. Butterfield who was one of the original collectors when the 'Cathedral Builders' was founded in 1925.

The death occurred of Sir Charles Morton (1853/1939) Joint Treasurer to the Executive Committee from 1918.

The Lady Chapel was re-pointed.

The asphalt roofs of the Ambulatory and Triforium were replaced with copper.

## 1940

On July 19th the statues of King George V and Queen Mary, the gift of Sir Frederick Radcliffe, were placed above the 'King's Porch'. It was so named, being the place where their Majesties, who had arrived at the Cathedral early, stood awaiting the clergy procession in 1924. The figures are the work of Edward Carter Preston.

In September on two consecutive nights high explosive bombs fell on the 'Founders Plot', some of the roofing was damaged and the door of the Children's Porch blown in. The effect of the explosion on the stained glass windows in the Lady Chapel and the South side of the Choir was serious, twelve windows being ruined beyond repair. The wrecked windows were boarded over with timber. As a result of the damage it was not possible to hold services in the Choir or Lady Chapel.

Early on the morning of Friday September 6th Mr. George Siddall, the engineer to the Dean and Chapter, was killed together with his wife Milly and daughter Christine by a bomb which exploded on their home in Washington Street situated near to the Cathedral. Their funeral service was held in the Cathedral on September 11th.

In November King George VI and Queen Elizabeth visited the Cathedral and inspected the damaged windows and the new part of the building. On leaving the Cathedral King George VI, said ' keep going whatever you do, even if you can only go on in a small way'.

On December 21st St Nicholas, the Parish Church of

# 1941

*On the night of May 5th a high explosive bomb hit the outer roof of the Derby Transept but was deflected by the brick transverse arch underneath.*

*Bomb damage*

GLW 617

*Leading Fireman George Brown.*

Liverpool, was hit by incendiary bombs during an air-raid and the main body of the Church was destroyed. Re-building began in 1949 and the new Church, dedicated to 'Our Lady and St Nicholas', was consecrated on October 18th 1952. The Chapel of St Peter commemorates the Church of St Peter which became the Pro-Cathedral in 1880. The Chapel contains a cross made from the charred timbers of the bombed Church which were rescued by the Rector the Revd D. Railton (1884/1955). The Revd Railton, who was a Military Chaplain during the First World War, was the originator of the idea of the tomb of the 'Unknown Warrior'.

The robing rooms beneath the Western Transept were used as public air-raid shelters.

As a result of the war the great Bourdon Bell was cast at Loughborough in the works of Messrs Taylor, the bell-founders. Amongst other works in the Diocese by the company are; St Nicholas Church, Liverpool, Southport Holy Trinity and the Hour Bell at Liverpool University, cast in 1892.

The Memorial Stone in memory of Dr. André John Melly, (1898/1936 ), the Liverpool born doctor who was leading the British Ambulance Service in Ethiopia when he was killed, was placed in the North Choir aisle. He was posthumously awarded the Albert Medal. The memorial stone, which graphically portrays the scene in which he lost his life, is the work of Edward Carter Preston. A Memorial Service for Dr. Melly was held at St Martins-in-the-Field, London, in which Archbishop Lang of Canterbury took part.

A new auxiliary organ console was installed. It was positioned on the North side of the crossing of the Eastern Transept. The photographic copy of the 'Roll of Honour' was transferred from the left to the right side of the Memorial Transept arch.

On December 10th the death occurred of the first Lord Vestey (1859/1940) who, with his brother Sir Edmund Vestey (1866/1953), financed the building of the tower.

The death occurred of Canon William Thompson Elliott. He was the first Sub-Dean of the Cathedral and one of the founder members of the 'Cathedral Builders', which was launched in 1925. From 1926 to 1938 he was Vicar of Leeds Parish Church and from 1938 to his death he was Canon of Westminster Abbey. His funeral took place in the Abbey where his ashes were laid to rest in the Inskip Chapel.

The architect presented to the Executive Committee his designs for four pulpits, one on each of the main piers of the Tower arches

# 1941

On January 29th the Cathedral Commissioners submitted to His Majesty in Council a scheme for the Cathedral. This being the constitution and the statutes for the government of the Cathedral.

The Canon Treasurer became responsible for the care and charge of all treasures of the Cathedral and responsible for examining reports of the Cathedral surveyor, architect and clerk of works.

In February Admiral Sir Percy Noble, whose memorial is to be found in the North Choir aisle, opened his new headquarters at Derby House, Liverpool. As a result of the arrival of the 'Western Approaches Command' and as part of the welcome to the city Dean and Chapter ordered that the whole of the Cathedral was to be made available to any guests of the Command. The order instructed that the Chapter House was to be set apart for use by the Revd O.R.(Jimmy) Fulljames, R.N.V.R. Naval Chaplain on Merseyside to 'Western Approaches Command'. Visiting ships' Chaplains were also invited to make use of the Chapter House.

During May the city suffered considerable damage with a heavy loss of life. A period referred to as the 'May Blitz'.

On the night of May 5th a high explosive bomb hit the outer roof of the Derby Transept but was deflected by the brick transverse arch underneath. As a result the setting out shed was destroyed and the glass in the Timmis window in the South-East Transept was completely destroyed.

For his actions and bravery during this raid Auxiliary Fireman John Edmund Jones received the British Empire Medal. He also received recognition, along with Leading Fireman George Brown, for their services at the Cathedral. Both firemen received a silver medallion, the same medallion awarded by Sir Frederick Radcliffe to those who in 1934 had worked on the Cathedral site for ten years or more. Dean Dwelly presented the awards at Windsor Street A.F.S. Station and in his closing address to the fire crew, delivered the wishes of Sir Radcliffe,' to bind you up with the long history of the Cathedral for preservation is as important as building'.

The East clerestory window was also destroyed. The window, which was in memory of Barbara Ford, was replaced after the war in a blue 'mosaic' treatment by Carl Edwards. The name Ford does not appear in the replacement window. The West clerestory window of the South East Transept survived the bomb blast and contrasts markedly with the East clerestory window opposite. The window was donated by Thomas J. Walmsley, the ship owner, in memory of his mother

# 1942

*On September 20th the Royal Air Force 'Commemoration of the Battle of Britain Service' was held in the Cathedral.*

*Sir Frederick Radcliffe laying the Library Foundation Stone.*

Caroline Moody Walmsley (1836/1915). The damaged South Choir aisle annexe window was not replaced. The original window was in memory of the Singlehurst family.

The architect estimated £40,000 worth of war damage to the Cathedral, but about half of that was stained glass.

In May, Church House situated in Lord Street, was destroyed by enemy action. Many of the Cathedral committee records, papers and files were lost. The new Church House was situated at Moorfields.

On Saturday July 12th a Memorial Service was held for Dr. Francis Bernard Chavasse (1889/1941), who lost his life in a motoring accident. He was the son of Bishop Chavasse, the second Bishop of Liverpool. Dr. Chavasse was a leading ophthalmic surgeon and lecturer in ophthalmology at Liverpool University.

Sunday July 27th witnessed the dedication of the Central Space with the Western Transepts at the Service of 'Solemn Entrance in Time of War'. The architect, in admiration for their work read a 'Testimony to the Workers'. After the service the foundation stone for the Cathedral Liturgical Library bearing the name 'Radcliffe Library' was laid by Sir Frederick Radcliffe. The two storey block, which was to have included a refectory, was to have been situated at the East end of the Choir, however the building never came to fruition. The room above the Baptistery vestry was utilised as the Radcliffe library until 2009.

H.R.H. the Princess Royal and Mr. Wendell Wilkie (1892/1944), the American President's personal representative, visited the Cathedral.

Mr. Joseph Henry Harrod, Head Verger at the time of the consecration of the Lady Chapel in 1910, died at the age of 83. Known for his devotion to the Cathedral and for his humility his name is recorded on the 'treble bell' which is named *Bede.*

## 1942

The death occurred of Mr. Henry Sutton Timmis on January 25th. For 29 years he had served as a member of the Executive Committee. He donated the baptistery window in memory of his only son 2nd Lieut. Richard Sutton Timmis who died of the wounds he received in action near Ypres in 1915.

On February 20th Sir Giles Gilbert Scott positioned a stone on the north west pinnacle, which was one inch higher than its seven counterparts, on the octagonal tower summit. Also at the 'Topping Out' ceremony were Mr. Dudley Morrison; the contractor for building the Cathedral, Mr. Owen Pittaway; clerk

of works, Mr. W. Meredith; general foreman, Mr. Harry Oxon; the mason, Mr. Hugh Williams the fixer and Mr. Jack Hughes the labourer. Mr. James Dixon was the crane driver who lowered the finial into position. Carved into the stone is the date 1942 and Sir Giles' initials.

The Rt Revd William Temple (1881/1944), a former Bishop of Manchester, was installed Archbishop of Canterbury on April 17th. His father Frederick Temple (1801/1902) was also Archbishop of Canterbury from 1896 to 1902. A portrait of Archbishop William Temple is to be found in the *Bishops'* window.

On Monday July 13th the architect's mother, Mrs. Ellen Gilbert Scott, made her first visit to the Cathedral.

On September 20th the Royal Air Force 'Commemoration of the Battle of Britain Service' was held in the Cathedral.

In December a 'Day of Mourning and Prayer' was held for the victims of mass massacres of Jews. Archbishop Temple of Canterbury was one of the founders, in 1942, of The Council of Christians and Jews.

The reredos in the War Memorial Chapel was improved by the gilding of some of the carvings and mouldings. Riddel-posts were also installed.

As a result of the use being made, for devotional purposes, by the 'Western Approaches Command', structural alterations were made to the Chapter House. They consisted of an Altar against the North wall, with riddel-posts and hangings and a carved frame from which hung a gilded wooden cross to suggest a reredos (in 1997 the Cross was moved to the right of the Holy Table to accommodate Aitchison's painting *Calvary).* In addition a predella, on which the minister stands when presiding at the Eucharist, was constructed. A close friendship ensued between Sir Max Horton, Commander-in-Chief of Western Approaches and Dean Dwelly.

Together they encouraged the promotion of the spiritual welfare of officers and the men and women who came to look upon the Cathedral as the 'Parish Church of the Western Approaches'.

The ashes of Lt General Sir Hugh Jeudwine (1862/1942) were laid to rest below the memorial stone to the 55th West Lancashire Division, which he commanded during the First World War. It was on Sir Jeudwine's command that the motto 'They win or die who wear the rose of Lancaster' was to encircle the division sign.

The plans for the West elevation were published. The design included a *porte-cochère.*

# 1944

*The Order of Merit was conferred on Sir Giles Gilbert Scott by King George VI.*

*Rt Revd Clifford Arthur Martin the fourth Bishop of Liverpool.*

## 1943

In January the crown of the tower was revealed. To celebrate the occasion a tribute luncheon was held at Liverpool's Stork Hotel.

On January 2nd the 17th Festival of Cathedral Builders Service was held. Canon J.S. Bezzant in his sermon declared 'the Cathedral will outlast the centuries and be a daily inspiration to the stream of people who pass it by '.

On Sunday July 11th a Service was held in the Cathedral for the recently formed Liverpool Sea Cadet Corps.

Archdeacon George John Howson (1854/1943) who served on the Executive Committee from 1916 died. Archdeacon Howson, who was the son of the Very Revd John Howson, Dean of Chester, (1867/1885), spent the greater part of his ministry in the Diocese of Liverpool. In 1927 with his friend William Bunn he created a bird sanctuary in St James' cemetery.

The death occurred of Major Hugh Duncan Woodsend (1896/1943) a member of the Executive Committee and secretary of 'Cathedral Builders' from 1936 to 1939.

## 1944

On April 15th Bishop David resigned. He was succeeded by the Rt Revd Clifford Arthur Martin as the fourth Bishop of Liverpool. Bishop Martin had previously been Vicar of St Andrews, Plymouth, where he had also served as Chaplain to King George VI.

On St. Georges Day April 23rd, Dean Dwelly welcomed to the Cathedral, Firemen and Police Constables who had received honours for their actions and bravery during the 'May Blitz'.

On the morning of July 12th the funeral service, with full naval honours, was held in the Cathedral for Captain F. J. Walker (1896/1944), who played such an important role in the Battle of the Atlantic during the Second World War. Following the service, his coffin was borne down to the River Mersey and then on to HMS *Hesperus* before being buried at sea in sight of the Bootle Docks. Sir Max Horton, Commander, Western Approaches, who read the oration, declared 'the Western Approaches shall be his tomb'. On October 16th 1998 a statue of Captain Walker was unveiled by the Duke of Edinburgh at Liverpool Pierhead. The memorial was dedicated to Captain Walker, the men of his 36th Escort and the 2nd Support Group, and all those who fought in the Battle of the Atlantic.

On Sunday July 16th the B.B.C. broadcast a talk on Liverpool Cathedral under the title *Forty Years a-Growing.* Sir Giles Gilbert Scott contributed to the broadcast.

On Sunday morning September 10th Bishop Martin was installed Bishop of Liverpool by Dean Dwelly. The congregation included The Earl of Sefton, Lord Mayor of Liverpool, and other civic dignitaries.

Canon T. Arthur E. Davey (1891/1944) Canon Residentiary from 1931, died on October 29th. His ashes were placed in the Chapel of the Holy Spirit where there is an inscribed memorial stone.

The erection of the font, which is of Lunel Rubane marble, was completed. It was the gift of Miss Brancker. The figures of the twelve apostles were carved in low relief by Edward Carter Preston. The oak baldachino, the gift of Mrs. Neilson and the oak font cover the gift of Mr. Pegram, were carved by Messrs Green and Vardy of London. The colouring and decoration of the ceiling of the baldachino was carried out by Watts & Co of London. The first child to be baptised in the font was Louise Juliette Gilbert Scott on April 28th 1951, the granddaughter of the architect.

The Order of Merit was conferred on Sir Giles Gilbert Scott by King George VI.

Miss Bickersteth retired from the position of Secretary of the 'Cathedral Builders'. She was succeeded by Mr. Joseph Forrester.

Edward Carter Preston's carved group, which illustrates the story of 'Christ calling the little children to Him', was placed in the tympanum over the interior of the Baptistery doorway. The child figures were modelled by his four daughters.

The processional emblems (in the shape of the Chapter Seal) which indicate turning or halting points were marked into the floor in the Choir, immediately in front of the Sanctuary steps and into the floor in the Western Transept where the North/South and East/West axis intercept.

A committee of Anglican, Roman Catholic, and Free Church members was formed to take on the task of rebuilding bombed churches.

## 1945

In April the doors between the Baptistery and the Rankin Porch were put in place. They were the gift of the children of Robert Gladstone (1866/1940), the first Deputy Chairman of the Executive Committee. He was also Chairman of the Mersey Docks and Harbour Board from 1899 to 1911. Gladstone Dock is named after him. As one of the original members of the Cathedral Committee his portrait appears in the *Laymen's* window.

Mr. Harold Carleton Walker died on April 2nd. He joined the Executive Committee in 1927 and was joint

# 1945

*On May 8th Prime Minister Winston Churchill (1874/1965) announced that 'the German war is at an end'. Liverpool people came to the Cathedral to express their joy and thankfulness in an act of common worship.*

*Field Marshall Montgomery visiting the Cathedral in 1945.*

*Neilson memorial in the Lady Chapel.*

Honorary Treasurer with Sir Charles Morton from 1935. His ashes lie in the North Choir aisle where there is an inscribed stone in the pavement.

On May 8th Prime Minister Winston Churchill (1874/1965) announced that 'the German war is at an end'. Liverpool people came to the Cathedral to express their joy and thankfulness in an act of common worship.

During the Second World War work on the building of the Cathedral was never wholly stopped. However the workforce, which numbered over two hundred in 1939, had been reduced to thirty five in 1945.

On Saturday June 9th to celebrate the twentieth anniversary of the foundation of 'Cathedral Builders' Archbishop Garbett of York, gave the sermon.

Mrs. Helen Swift Neilson (1869/1945) wife of Francis Neilson, died in June. Mrs. Neilson and her husband were both generous benefactors to the Cathedral and in 1949 the Francis Neilson Trust Fund was established to assist the maintenance of the Cathedral music department. A Memorial Stone to the memory of Helen is situated in the Narthex of the Lady Chapel. The panel which is of Hopton wood was designed by Sir Giles Gilbert Scott and executed by Edward Carter Preston. Helen who was born in America recorded in her family history, *My Father and My Mother* (1937), that her ancestry went back to the 17th century Swyfte family of Rotherham, Yorkshire. On her visits to England she would visit All Saints Church, Rotherham where her ancestors are buried.

A 'Youth and United Nations Service' was held on

June 11th in the presence of Archbishop Garbett of York, Sir Max Horton and Air Vice-Marshall Sir Leonard Slatter.

A service of 'Recollection of the Western Approaches' led by Archbishop Garbett of York was held on Thursday August 9th. A scroll, of blue morocco leather, containing the names of the six thousand and eighty one who gave their lives during the war was received into the keeping of the Cathedral. Colonel in Chief, Admiral Sir Max Horton set his mark on the Western transept.

On Saturday September 15th a Coastal Command Memorial Service was held. At the 'Service of Celebration' the Dean led the company to the Corona Gallery where Senior Air Staff Officer Scarlett-Streatfield, who died in action, was remembered. In 1994 the 'Battle of the Atlantic' memorial case, given in memory of Vice Admiral Sir Peter Gretton (1912/1992), was dedicated by Bishop Sheppard. The case was designed by Mr. Keith Scott.

The Rt Revd Geoffrey Fisher (1887/1972), a former Bishop of Chester, was appointed Archbishop of Canterbury. In 1960 Archbishop Fisher visited Pope John XXIII, which was the first meeting between an Archbishop of Canterbury and a Pope since the English Reformation.

A R.A.F Service held in the Cathedral included a reading from Francis Brett Young's (1884/1954) epic poem *The Island*. Published in 1944 the poem recounts in verse the history of Britain from the Bronze Age to the Battle of Britain. Francis died in 1954 and his ashes rest in Worcester Cathedral.

# 1946

*On January 9th a Memorial Service for Miss Eleanor Rathbone (1872/1946), the Independent M.P. and campaigner for women's rights, who died on January 2nd, was held in the Cathedral.*

The heating was switched from oil to gas.

At the request of the Timmis family an inscription was carved into the sanctuary floor (on the South side) 'to the memory of John Dunston Sutton Timmis accidently killed November 8th 1931. William Sutton Brown D.S.O. Major Cold Stream Guards died from wounds July 28th 1944. Grandsons of Thomas Sutton Timmis and Caroline Anne Timmis.

Mr. Stanley Williams, who joined the Cathedral staff in 1931 as a verger, was appointed Clerk to the Dean, a position he held until his retirement in 1980, completing almost half a century of work in the Cathedral.

## 1946

Work commenced to repair the damage incurred by the Cathedral during the war.

On January 9th a Memorial Service for Miss Eleanor Rathbone (1872/1946), the Independent M.P. and campaigner for women's rights, who died on January 2nd, was held in the Cathedral. Eleanor was the daughter of William Rathbone V1 (1819/1902) and Emily Rathbone (Lyle). The family home was at Greenbank, Liverpool. The address was given by Sir James Mountford. The *Hymnologists'* window commemorates the Rathbone family which, for more than two hundred and fifty years, had been closely associated with the public, educational and philanthropic life of the city.

Mr. Walter Gilbert (1871/1946) the sculptor, craftsman in metal and founder of the Bromsgrove Guild, whose best known work in the Cathedral are the figures on the Choir Reredos, died in January. A bust of Walter Gilbert, by his son Donald, is exhibited at Hartlebury Museum, Worcester.

Miss Rosalie Eleanor Stolterfoht, who founded the Cathedral Embroidery Association, died in February. Miss Stolterfoht worked and presented to the Cathedral all the frontals in both the Choir and Lady Chapel, and in addition the sanctuary hangings in the Lady Chapel and the 'fair linen'. The Elizabeth Hoare Embroidery Gallery, which is on the third floor of the Cathedral, was opened in 1992 and is devoted to ecclesiastical embroidery. The gallery was founded by Sir Giles Gilbert Scott's niece Elizabeth Hoare (1916/2001) the owner of Watts & Co, the makers of ecclesiastical vestments.

In April Mr. T. Stone jun. was appointed Honorary Secretary to the 'Cathedral Builders'.

On Passion Sunday the Revd Charles R. Claxton (1903/1992) was consecrated Bishop Suffragan of Warrington, the first occasion on which such a service had been held in the Cathedral. The consecration was performed by Archbishop Garbett of York. Bishop Claxton lived in Halsall where he was also Rector until 1958. He was the last Bishop of Warrington to combine the running of a parish with the work of a Suffragan. He later served as Bishop of Blackburn from 1960 to 1971.

On Saturday May 12th an oaken casket containing an illuminated 'Roll of Honour', in memory of those who lost their lives serving in the National Fire Service during the Second World War, was placed in the Sanctuary of the Cathedral.

*Work commenced to repair the damage incurred by the Cathedral during the war.*

# 1947

*From January 21st the country experienced a severe cold spell with large drifts of snow, conditions which only eased in mid-March. As a result, during February and March, work on the Cathedral was suspended.*

*The Vestey Coat of Arms.*

In August Dean Dwelly received into the Cathedral the National Fire Service flag.

A catafalque and four stools were presented to the Cathedral by Lord Samuel Vestey in memory of his son Capt. William Howarth Vestey (1912/1944) of the 1st Battalion Scots Guards, who was killed on active service near Lake Bolsena, Italy, on June 26th 1944. He is buried in Bolsena War Cemetery and is also commemorated in the churchyard of St. Michael's Church, Yanworth, Gloucester.

New figures of St John the Baptist and Moses sculpted by Edward Carter Preston were placed in the niches on the pulpit. They replaced earlier ones which the architect considered to be unsatisfactory. They were the gift of the Liverpool Women's War Service Bureau. A paving stone on the North side of the pulpit is inscribed; 'Be speak their thankfulness the ways and love of the spirit of true service 1914-1948'.

The *Spirit of Service* window in the South wall of the East Transept, destroyed in 1941, was restored.

New stalls for the Dean and Chapter were placed in the Chapter House.

Mr. Herbert Hendrie (1887/1946) who designed and executed all the stained glass in the North West and South West transepts died. Born in Manchester he joined the College of Art in Edinburgh in 1921 but continued to do freelance work.

## 1947

From January 21st the country experienced a severe cold spell with large drifts of snow, conditions which only eased in mid-March. As a result, during February and March, work on the Cathedral was suspended.

The St John window and St Mark window in the South Choir aisle, damaged in 1941, were re-glazed. The work was carried out by James Powell & Sons (Whitefriars) Ltd. The redesigned St John window was James Hogan's last work in the Cathedral.

The war-damaged stone work on the South side of the Cathedral, particularly surrounding the 'Founders' Plot' and 'Children's Porch', was repaired. The scaffolding surrounding the tower was removed.

The three pairs of outer doors of the Rankin Porch, designed by the architect, were fitted. The making of the doors, which commenced in 1941, was carried out by joiners at the Morrison joiners' shop in Wavertree. The team led by Mr. W. Christian were Mr. R. Ogden, Mr. J. Lindsay and Mr. J. Ogden.

Miss Amy Smith, Mr. Robert Martin and Mr. Herbert

Smith defrayed the cost of the inner doors of the Rankin porch in memory of Nelly Smith (1873/1932) 'who worked for the cause of temperance in this city'.

The inscription on the North wall of the under-tower, in memory of the Vestey family who donated the tower, was unveiled. The donors' names are not given, they being merely described as the survivors of a family of eight sons and four daughters.

The ashes of Lord William Vestey (1859/1940) were laid to rest under a simple slab of black marble on which is carved his coat of arms. The carving which, embodies the family's interest in the meat trade, cold storage, and shipping by the use of a bull, sheep and an iceberg floating in the sea, was carved by Edward Carter Preston. Inscribed is the motto; *E Labore Stabilitas* (from labour stability).

All the windows in the Cathedral were cleaned inside and out.

Sir Arthur Stanley (1869/ 1947), third son of the 16th Earl of Derby and an original member of the Executive Committee died. He was M.P. for Ormskirk 1898 to 1918. His coat of arms and those of John H. Burrell, Grandmasters of the West Lancashire Province, are carved in the spandrels of the turret doorway of the Chapter House. Sir Arthur Stanley is featured in the *Laymen's* window.

## 1948

On January 12th the death occurred of Mr. James H. Hogan (1883/1948) the stained glass designer who worked on the windows from the early days of the Cathedral's construction. He was art director, chief designer and managing director of Powells (Whitefriars). The Old and New Testament windows are considered to be his finest. As a tribute to him Carl Edwards, a former pupil of James, included a portrait of him in the *Laymen's* window.

The screens were taken off the restored St John Window.

On Saturday March 13th at Liverpool Stadium, St Pauls Square, Field Marshall Earl Wavell of Cyrenaica, patron of the Chindits Old Comrades Association, delivered 'The Patron's Charge' to the Chindits. In the Cathedral on the following day Bishop Martin, in the presence of Mrs. Lorna Wingate widow of Major General Orde Wingate (1903/1944), dedicated the Chindit Flag which hangs in the War Memorial Chapel.

On May 30th a Festival Service for the Royal Institute of British Architects was held in the Cathedral. The Institute was founded for the advancement of architecture under its charter granted in 1837. The

# 1949

*On Tuesday March 29th the Rankin Porch was opened by H.R.H. Princess Elizabeth who was making her first visit to the Cathedral.*

Royal Gold Medal, first awarded in 1848 for outstanding contribution to international architecture, was awarded to Sir Giles Gilbert Scott in 1925. The R.I.B.A. banner hangs in the South East transept.

A severe thunderstorm on July 31st removed one of the pinnacles on the South-East corner of the Tower. Some four feet of the top were completely removed.

The death occurred of the 17th Earl of Derby (1865/1948) who for forty years had acted as President of the Cathedral Executive Committee. He played a leading role in 1924 with the arrangements for the consecration of the Cathedral. A Conservative politician, in August 1914 he organised the recruitment of 1500 Liverpool men to form 'pals battalions'. He was succeeded by his grandson Edward Stanley 18th Earl of Derby (1918/1994).

The Liverpool & District Sheepdog Society presented to the Cathedral a Bishop's Crozier made in wood.

Mr. Ronald Woan, who sang as a chorister at the consecration of the Cathedral, was appointed Director of the Choir in succession to Mr. E. C. Robinson who retired after 24 years as choirmaster. Mr. Woan served for thirty four years and retired as Director of Music in 1982.

The death occurred of Miss Lillie Reed the sculptress who sculpted the figures on the Children's Porch.

The main work on the tower was completed. In addition the repair of the war damage was also finished.

A limited licence was granted to start work on the First Bay of the Nave.

In November excavation and work on the foundations for the construction of the first Nave began.

## 1949

A Memorial Service was held on January 30th for Tommy Handley (1892/ 1949) the Liverpool born comedian whose radio show ITMA (*'Its That Man Again'*) kept the nation laughing during the Second World War. It was recorded that the crowds attending the Service were 'the greatest ever known at the Cathedral'. A Memorial Service was also held at St Paul's, London.

Mr. Noel Rawsthorne was appointed assistant organist to Dr. Henry Goss Custard.

On Tuesday March 29th the Rankin Porch was opened by H.R.H Princess Elizabeth who was making her first visit to the Cathedral. Choir boy Jeffrey Holiday presented to Her Royal Highness a cushion on which lay the 'golden' key to open the door. To commemorate her visit, in which she was accompanied by the Duke of Edinburgh, the monograms 'E' and 'P' entwined with a true 'Lovers Knot' were carved on the first pier of the Nave. Choristers Kevin Lavelle and Peter Smith held the stencil whilst the Princess dipped the brush in the white paint to trace her initial. The inscription was carved by the sculptor Mr. Tom Murphy.

H.R.H Princess Elizabeth presented the Gold Albert Medal of the Royal Society of Arts to Sir Giles Gilbert Scott. The citation reads 'Builder of a lasting heritage

*H.R.H. Princess Elizabeth who was making her first visit to the Cathedral, opens the Rankin Porch.*

# 1951

*April 24th heralded the arrival of 'Great George', the Cathedral's huge Bourdon Bell, the second largest bell in England.*

*Louise Juliette Scott the architect's granddaughter, the first person to be baptised in the font.*

for Britain'. Princess Elizabeth said 'Your name will always be remembered with Liverpool Cathedral which, in my opinion, ranks in splendour with the Cathedrals of the Middle Ages and will take its place amongst Europe's greatest monuments'.

The death occurred of Lady Louise Wallbank Scott (1888/1949) the wife of Sir Giles Gilbert Scott. Lady Louise was buried in a grave outside the Cathedral.

On September 18th the RAF Ensign, a gift of 1843 airmen recruits, was presented to the Cathedral after their visit whilst in training at RAF station West Kirby.

A United Church Service was held on October 30th.

The pinnacle struck by lightning in 1948 was replaced

Laurence Davies' talks to the choristers took place every Sunday between 1.30pm and 2.30pm in the Chapter House.

The new windows on the South side of the Lady Chapel and the new Annunciation window on the Lady Chapel gallery, which were destroyed during the Second World War, were replaced. The designs were by James Hogan whilst the actual glass was the work of Carl Edwards.

## 1950

A Service to mark the centenary of the Liverpool Chamber of Commerce was held on February 5th. The sermon was given by Archbishop Garbett of York and the Service was followed by a reception at Liverpool Town Hall. The Chamber was formed by a group of local merchants, led by Leone Levi (1821/1888), who in 1844 left Italy, his birthplace, to settle in Liverpool.

On December 24th the death occurred, at his home in Cornwall, of the third Bishop of Liverpool, the Rt Revd Albertus Augustus David (1867/1950).

The name of the editor of the *Liverpool Cathedral Bulletin,* Colonel Vere. E. Cotton, was revealed for the first time in the December edition, which completed twenty five years of publication.

The Reredos was vacuum cleaned for the first time since its erection.

At the 'Cathedral Builders' service a large silver alms dish, in memory of John Rankin Rathbone (1910/1940) and Henry Nicholas Rathbone (1913/1942) who died in the Second World War, was presented by their brother William Rathbone. They were the sons of William Rathbone VIII (1880/1941). Their mother Agnes was the daughter of John Rankin of the ship owning family who donated the Rankin porch.

A gate known as the 'Traitors Gate' was fixed at the Western entrance to the Cathedral.

Canon Cyril Frederick Twitchett (1890/1950) Archdeacon of Liverpool and member of the Executive Committee from 1933, died. His ashes were placed in the Chapel of the Holy Spirit where his name is inscribed on the paving. He was succeeded by the Revd Hubert Wilkinson, formerly Archdeacon of Westmorland and Furness.

The death occurred of Mrs. Mary Dwelly wife of Dean Dwelly.

## 1951

On January 6th the funeral of the Rt Revd Albert Augustus David took place in the Cathedral. His ashes were placed at the foot of the pier, to the east of the Bishop's throne, which he had marked with a Cross of Consecration on July 19th 1924. The memorial stone includes the last line from the Vulgate version of I Corinthians chapter 2 verse 10; *Spiritus Scrutateur Profunda Dei* ('for the Spirit searcheth all things, yea, the deep things of God').

April 24th heralded the arrival of 'Great George', the Cathedral's huge Bourdon Bell, the second largest bell in England. The giant bell has a diameter of nine feet six inches and weighs fourteen and a half tons. It was the gift of William Baron Vestey of Kingswood and his wife Evelyn with Sir Edmund Hoyle Vestey and his wife Ellen, in memory of King George V.

On April 28th Louise Juliette Gilbert Scott, the architect's granddaughter, was the first person to be baptised in the Font.

May 4th witnessed 'Great George' being hoisted into position. The task of placing the bourdon bell in the belfry commenced at 8.35am and was completed at 8.12pm in the presence of Dean Dwelly and company. The clapper was unlashed and 'Great George' was tolled at 9.00pm precisely.

The bell, which was cast by Messrs Taylor of Loughborough, was dedicated by Bishop Martin on Sunday June 17th the 50th anniversary of the historic meeting in Liverpool Town Hall. In the bell ringing chamber were Messrs; Brennan, Douglas, Lavelle, Newton, Rimmer and Smith. A Service of Thanksgiving was held on the following day attended by the Lord Mayor of Liverpool, Col Vere Egerton Cotton. *The Daily Post* published a special supplement to mark the jubilee.

The architect exhibited his plans for the West front.

On July 17th the ashes of Lady Mary Grace Jeudwine, widow of General Sir Hugh Jeudwine, were placed

# 1952

*On February 5th the death of King George VI (1895/1952) was announced and on February 18th a Memorial Service was held in the Cathedral.*

*May 4th 1951 witnessed 'Great George' being hoisted into position.*

with those of her husband, who died in 1942, in a niche behind the 55th Division Memorial, in the South arm of the Eastern Transept.

On August 9th the funeral of Admiral Sir Max Horton (1883/1951) took place in the Cathedral with full naval honours. At the service the King was represented by Captain Sir Harold Campbell, the Prime Minister by Sir John G. Lang and Mr. Churchill by Rear-Admiral P. Kekewich. His ashes were placed in the South arm of the Eastern Transept at the foot of the North-East pier.

On the morning of Saturday November 17th the Cathedral bells were pealed for the first time in the presence, and on the command of H.R.H Princess Elizabeth. The Princess accompanied by Prince Philip had disembarked at Liverpool in the morning from the *Empress of Scotland,* after their tour in Canada and the United States. Geoffrey Bethel a chorister presented the Princess with a bouquet of Lancashire roses. The Cathedral Cross Guild Ringers for the first 'short touch' of the bells were; Roy Brennan, David Craine, John Elsworth, Roland Eveleigh, Donald Gadsby, Kevin Lavelle and Peter Smith. They were assisted by other members of the Cross Guild Ringers. Mr. George R. Newton, the Ringing Master, who had 50 years' bell-ringing experience all over the country was presented with a hand-bell by the Merseyside ringers who took part in the welcoming ceremony. As revealed on the tenor bell, named by Bishop David, *Emmanuel,* the cost of the ring of thirteen bells was defrayed from a bequest made in 1912 by Mr. Thomas Bartlett (1839/1912) a Liverpool wine merchant. The 13 bells which encircle the bourdon bell were manufactured by Messrs. Mears and Stainbank at their Whitechapel foundry, London. A portrait of Mr. Albert A. Hughes, who attended 'The Hallowing', a senior partner in the firm when the Bartlett Ring was cast, appears in the *Laymen's* Window.

Mr. A.G. Crimp, manager to Sir Giles Gilbert Scott, retired. He was succeeded by Mr. F.G. Thomas.

As part of Liverpool's contribution to the 'Festival of Britain', which was opened on May 6th on the south bank of the Thames in London , the Dean and Chapter staged two exhibitions. One in the Lady Chapel, which dealt with the design and making of stained glass, the other in the Oratory (at that time owned by the Cathedral Building Committee) which contained an exhibition of photographs and models of the building of the Cathedral. Also on display were Edward Carter Preston's original models for all the sculpture in the under-tower and West end of the Cathedral. The model of the original design, with twin towers, was shown for the first time in twenty five years. Also on display was a stained glass panel, the work of Alfred Fisher an apprentice window artist and member of the Cross Guild. The panel, which commemorates the

ringing of the bells on November 17th, shows two bells with the etched initials of Dean Dwelly and the names of those who rang the bells.

The Vestey Tower was completed.

For the first time power tools were installed in the masons' yard. For fifty years all the work, apart from sawing the stones, was done by hand. Further mechanisation followed in 1954 with the introduction of moulding and planing machines.

The inner doors of the Rankin porch which are of English oak, elaborately carved and studded with bronze paterea, were fitted. They were made by Messrs. Green & Vardy of London. The bronze grill, across the outside entrance to the porch, was manufactured by James Gibbons Ltd.

The bronze grille to the Children's Porch of the Lady Chapel was completed.

## 1952

On February 5th the death of King George VI (1895/1952) was announced and on February 18th a Memorial Service was held in the Cathedral. Civic Services to commemorate the life of His Majesty were held throughout the Diocese.

Mr. Harry E Goodlad (1892/1952), Head Steward and member of the General Committee died on March 2nd. His ashes lie in the North Choir aisle, where his name is inscribed on the floor.

On April 26th the death occurred of Canon C.F.H. Soulby (1881/1952) the Cathedral Guest Master and the Dean's Proctor. He was known as an inspired guide 'who always had something fresh and appropriate to say'. His ashes were laid to rest near to the North side of the Sanctuary, by the bronze gate leading to the North Choir aisle, where a carved inscription in his memory is to be found on the marble floor.

To celebrate the Very Revd F.W. Dwelly's 21 years as Dean of Liverpool, on Sunday October 6th the Cross Guild Ringers rang a peal of bells to mark the occasion. After Matins, about 90 Guild members assembled in the Chapter House where the Dean was presented with a manuscript copy of an *Evening Service* written by Christopher le Fleming one of his favourite composers. Dean Dwelly described the occasion as 'one of the greatest days in my life'.

The Revd Frederick W. Dillistone, Professor of Theology at the Episcopal Divinity School, Cambridge was appointed Canon and Chancellor on the resignation of Canon James S. Bezzant, who took up the post of lecturer in divinity at Cambridge University.

# 1953

*Paul McCartney failed his audition for the Cathedral choir, being turned down by Ronald Woan the Cathedral choirmaster.
In 2008 Sir Paul presented his Liverpool Oratorio in the Cathedral.*

A replica of some of the crown jewels were put on show in the Cathedral prior to the coronation of Her Majesty Queen Elizabeth.

A moveable oak screen was presented to the Cathedral by members of the Liverpool Branch of the Royal College of Nursing in memory of Mary Jones their Chairperson from 1928 to 1952 and President of the R.C.N. during the years 1940/1942.

The Chair lift, which was built by the Express Lift Company, was completed.

## 1953

On January 28th the death occurred of Mr. Edgar C. Robinson (1877/1953) the Cathedral's first choirmaster. Mr. Robinson, who was an organist and composer, was assistant organist at Lincoln Cathedral 1895/1899, organist at Gainsborough Parish Church 1899/1906, and organist at All Saints, Wigan 1906/1919. His named is carved into the pavement in the North Choir aisle where his ashes lie.

A Service to mark the Coronation of Her Majesty Queen Elizabeth on May 31st was held in the Cathedral.

On the Wednesday and Thursday of Coronation week, Mr. Malcolm Saville (1901/1982), the children's author, visited the Cathedral and at two services 1500 school children were given a specially written *Coronation Souvenir Booklet* by the author. The Cross Guild boys had lunch with Dean Dwelly at the Adelphi Hotel, where they presented Mr. Saville with a Chorister's Guild coronation mug.

The Festival Service of Cathedral Builders was held on Saturday July 18th when the preacher was Bishop Michael Gresford Jones of St Albans. Bishop Michael served at St Albans from 1950 to 1970 when he was succeeded by Bishop Robert Runcie (1921/2000) who was born in Great Crosby, Merseyside. As Archbishop Runcie of Canterbury in March 1982, at the Parish Church of Liverpool, he was forced to abandon a speech when shouted down by those angry about Pope John Paul's prospective visit to Liverpool.

In September the death occurred of the Cathedral President Sir Frederick M. Radcliffe (1861/1953), of whom it was said, if Sir Giles has been the Napoleon of the Cathedral project, Sir Frederick has been the Carnot, 'the organiser of victory'. A generous benefactor to the Cathedral his gift of the Radcliffe library, which consists of early and valuable printed books, is now housed at Liverpool Hope University. On September 29th a Memorial Service was held in the Cathedral. A memorial tablet to him and his wife Margaret, who died in 1955, is positioned beneath the *Church in England* window, behind which lie their

ashes. A further memorial to Sir Frederick is to be found in the North Choir aisle and his portrait appears in the *Laymen's* window.

On October 11th the King's Colour of the Plymouth Command G VI R was laid up in the West wall of the War Memorial Chapel.

Lord Derby was in attendance on Sunday October 25th and read the lesson at the service for the 'Laying up' of the Grenadier Guards 'Old Colours'.

Sir Edmund Vestey the donor, with his elder brother, of the Vestey tower, died on November 18th at the age of 87. His ashes were placed beside those of his brother the first Lord Vestey. An inscription was placed on the North wall of the undertower recording the fact that the ashes of the first Lord Vestey, and of his wife, rest near by.

The interior of the belfry was completed.

The remainder of the new windows on the North side of the Lady Chapel were completed.

Electric wiring which was 40 years old was replaced with pyrotenax insulated cable.

The hanging lanterns were repaired and regilded.

Mr. Owen Pittaway retired from his position as Clerk of Works. The Executive Committee presented him with an illuminated scroll to mark his 46 years of service. He was succeeded by Mr. H.V. James.

A knighthood was conferred upon Colonel Alan Tod, the Chairman of the Executive Committee, in recognition of his services to Liverpool in general and the Cathedral in particular.

An oak door between the staircase lobby and the South Nave aisle was donated in memory of Miss Henrietta Ellen Bailey, her father Dr. Francis James Bailey, her mother Mary Bailey and her brothers Dr. Francis W. Bailey and Dr Reginald T. Bailey. A window in the Radcliffe library was given by Mrs. Whitethread in memory of her daughter Miss Sarah Anne Whitethread who was one of the first collectors for 'Cathedral Builders.'

The death occurred, in her one hundredth year, of Mrs. Ellen Gilbert Scott, mother of the Cathedral architect.

The Baptistery window which had been damaged during the war was repaired.

The Archbishop of Canterbury, the Most Revd Geoffrey Fisher (1887/1972), conferred upon Mr. Goss Custard, the Cathedral organist, the degree of Doctor of Music at a private ceremony held in Lambeth College.

# 1954

*As part of the Cathedral's 'Jubilee' celebrations an exhibition of drawings, photographs, models and memorabilia was held in the newly restored Lady Chapel. It cost one shilling (5p) to enter.*

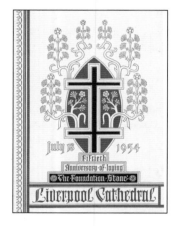

*The Order of Service booklet to celebrate the 50th Anniversary of the laying of the Foundation Stone.*

Paul McCartney failed his audition for the Cathedral choir, being turned down by Ronald Woan the Cathedral choirmaster. In 2008 Sir Paul presented his Liverpool *Oratorio* in the Cathedral. At the conclusion of the concert he commented, 'Got my own back', a remark much appreciated by the large audience.

## 1954

The 29th Festival Service of Cathedral Builders was held on July 17th when the preacher was Canon J.S. Bezzant, Dean of St John's College, Cambridge. Canon Bezzant's ministry commenced at Liverpool Cathedral in 1932 when he succeeded Canon C.E. Raven. Canon Bezzant left the Cathedral in 1952 to take up his appointment as Dean of St. John's College.

On the morning of July 18th, in the presence of the Archbishop Garbett of York, a Thanksgiving Service was held to mark the 50th Anniversary of the laying of the Foundation Stone. The 'Thanksgiving' was given by Bishop Chavasse of Rochester, son of Bishop Francis Chavasse, the founder of the Cathedral.

At Evensong, in an act of 'Remembrance and Thanksgiving', the names of the founders, benefactors, clergy and all those who had served and worked in the Cathedral were recalled.

Sir Alfred Shennan, Leader of the City Council and the Lord Mayor, Alderman A. Griffin, presented on behalf of the City Council a specially designed Processional Cross for use on civic occasions. The cross is the work of Mr. Leslie Durbin. At this time Mr. John Green acted as cross bearer.

The King's Regiment presented a silver vase engraved with the Regimental Crest.

As part of the Cathedral's 'Jubilee' celebrations an exhibition of drawings, photographs, models and memorabilia was held in the newly restored Lady Chapel. It cost one shilling (5p) to enter.
Dean Dwelly was honoured by the University of Liverpool with an honorary degree of Doctor of Laws.

To celebrate the commemoration of the laying of the Foundation Stone Lord Derby presented 20 *Prayer Books* and 20 copies of *Songs of Praise* bound in black morocco leather with the Chapter arms inset on the cover in silver and red.

Sir Alan and Lady Tod gave an oak stand for a processional cross.

Mr. Francis Neilson gave a number of books for the library, including a Coverdale Bible printed at Southwark in 1538. He also presented an original score copy of Handel's *Messiah* and a sixteenth century account book for the royal household.

Mr. Laurance Alfred Kent a mason-fixer for over twenty years died in October whilst working high up on the bay of the first Nave. His funeral service took place in the Cathedral on November 2nd.

On December 12th the Memorial tablet to Sir Frederick Radcliffe, which is incised in the wall of the North Choir aisle, was unveiled after the morning service by Dean Dwelly. The tablet was designed by Sir Giles Gilbert Scott. Sir Frederick's coat of arms, which displays the motto *no thorn no rose*, was carved by Edward Carter Preston.

The Executive Committee purchased 100 oak chairs.

The Chorister's Guild Fund was established by Dr. Francis Neilson. The object of the fund was 'to do good works for members of the Chorister's Guild'.

Two moulding and planing machines were installed in the masons' yard.

The Western Rooms were completed.

The death occurred of Harold Louis Swift (1882/1954), a memorial stone is to be found on the floor of the North Choir aisle where his ashes were laid to rest.

The staircases from the basement were paved with Lazenby stone from Cumbria. The stone has better wearing qualities for this purpose rather than the local Woolton stone.

## 1955

In March celebrations were held to mark the 75th anniversary of the creation of the Diocese.

Mr. Malcolm Watson West (1892/1955), the first bursar of the Cathedral, who served for twenty four years, died in April. A memorial stone is to be found in the North Choir aisle where his ashes were laid to rest. He was succeeded by Mr. T. E. Entwistle.
On Friday May 27th an appeal was launched to raise a sum of £500,000 for the building and endowment of the Cathedral. Sir Alan Tod was appointed Chairman of the Executive Committee. Bishop Chavasse of Rochester inaugurated the appeal.

On Sunday June 12th three colours of the King's Regiment (Liverpool) were laid up with others of the same regiment in the Memorial Transept. Known by the names of former owners, as the Cathcart and Hinde colours, they were delivered to the Dean by Lieut.- General Sir Alfred Dudley Ward (1905/1991), Colonel of the Regiment. He was Honorary Colonel of the University Training Corps (Liverpool 1951/1957).

The 1939-1945 War Memorial of the King's Regiment (Liverpool), in the form of a Book of Remembrance

# 1956

*The Revd Frederick W. Dillistone, Chancellor of the Cathedral, was installed the second Dean of Liverpool on April 11th.*

*Figure of the Apostle John, carved in low relief by Edward Carter Preston.*

containing the names of the 950 who lost their lives in the Second World War, was received from Brigadier R.N.M. Jones and dedicated by Bishop Martin. The sermon was given by Bishop Christopher Chavasse. The illuminated volume was designed and executed by Edward Carter Preston and Albert Carter Preston. Following the Thanksgiving Service the statues of King George VI and Queen Elizabeth, which flank the window above the Baptistery doorway, were unveiled by Lord Derby. The sculptured figures are the work of Edward Carter Preston and slightly larger than the figures opposite of King George V and Queen Mary. Above the door is a shield bearing, beneath a crown, the royal initials entwined by a tasselled cord.

In June the 'Visitors Verge' was presented in memory of Richard Walker (1880/1953), by his wife and daughters.

On July 17th at the 'Cathedral Builders' Festival Service the preacher was the Suffragan Bishop of Croyden the Rt Revd Cuthbert Bardsley (1907/1991). In 1956 he was translated to the Diocese of Coventry where he served, until 1976, with much distinction and playing a major part in the building of the new Coventry Cathedral. Bishop Bardsley also preached in Liverpool Cathedral in November 1979 when representatives of all the parishes in the Diocese presented 'pledges' of their centenary plans and financial thank offering. A memorial to Bishop Bardsley, who was related to the first Archdeacon of Warrington, Canon John Wareing Bardsley, is situated in Coventry Cathedral.

Dean Dwelly retired in September.

Bishop Gresford Jones retired from his Canonry at the end of September.

In October the tower was formally handed over to the Dean and Chapter.

On Christmas Day the Lady Chapel was used for the first time since 1940.

The death was announced of Bernard Vardy (1886/1955). He was responsible for some of the finest woodwork in the Cathedral, notably the carved oak baldachino over the font. He worked closely with Sir Giles Gilbert Scott on the restoration of the House of Commons and the Guild Hall after the Second World War.

The Dulverton Trust donated £25,000 to defray the cost of the Arch across the eastern end of the Nave. The trust was founded in 1949 by the 1st Lord Dulverton, Sir Gilbert A. H. Wills (1880/1956) who was President of the Imperial Tobacco Company.

Miss Jean Clayton and Miss Gwen Clayton presented a mace to be used by the Dean in memory of their mother Helen J. Clayton (1872/1952). The mace was designed and executed by Leslie Durbin.

Dr. Henry Goss Custard, after holding office for 38 years, retired as organist. He was succeeded by the deputy organist Noel Rawsthorne who, at the age of 25 years, was the youngest Cathedral organist in the country. Noel was Cathedral organist for twenty five years and when he retired in 1980 the Dean and Chapter, to mark his distinguished service, conferred upon him the honorary title *Organist Emeritus*.

Lady Vestey presented a record player to the Choristers Guild.

# 1956

The Revd Frederick W. Dillistone, Chancellor of the Cathedral, was installed the second Dean of Liverpool on April 11th.

A Civic Cross Mace, made of silver and walnut, was presented by Mrs. Barker in memory of her husband Ernest. His name appears on the crown-piece together with the inscription 'He loved humanity'. It was used for the first time on July 21st during the service commemorating the 52nd anniversary of the laying of the foundation stone. Also used for the first time was the new 'Beadle' which is carried before the civic cross.

During July the Corona Gallery was open to visitors of an evening.

In December work commenced on the erection of the Nave Arch. One of principal masons on the construction of the Arch was Mr. John Rowbottom.

Sir Giles Gilbert Scott presented a piano to the Cross Guild.

Mrs. Crosthwaite presented a silver flower bowl in memory of her husband Alderman Arthur Crosthwaite who died in 1925. He was Lord Mayor of Liverpool in 1901 and opened the proceedings at the meeting on June 17th when the resolution to build a Cathedral was passed.

The Memorial Tablet, which is situated in the North choir aisle, to Admiral Sir Percy Noble (1880/1955), Commander-in-Chief of Royal Navy's Western Approach Command, was dedicated by Bishop Martin at a service in the presence of his sons Commander Allan Noble M.P. and Captain Charles Noble RN. Admiral Noble hoisted his flag in February 1941, when he opened the headquarters at Derby House, Liverpool, where he served until 1942. The memorial tablet which is of Italian limestone was designed by Edward Carter Preston.

# 1957

*On May 9th at the age of 76 years the death occurred of the Very Revd Frederick W. Dwelly, first Dean of Liverpool. A congregation of 2,000 attended the funeral service on May13th which was conducted by Bishop Martin.*

*Memorial tablet by Edward Carter Preston to Admiral Sir Max Horton. In the foreground the Cope Chest.*

Canon Basil Naylor was installed Chancellor of the Cathedral. After war service as a Chaplain in the Royal Navy he became a fellow of St. Peter's College, Oxford where he was tutor in theology. He also served as Diocesan Director of Ordinands and Director of Training until his retirement in 1982. Canon Naylor died in 1988 and his ashes were laid to rest in the South Choir aisle. His epitaph incised into the memorial stone reads; 'Scholar. Liturguist. Musician'.

The offices of the Diocese moved to 1 Hanover Street, Liverpool. The premises were previously occupied by the Mersey Mission to Seamen.

## 1957

On May 9th at the age of 76 years the death occurred of the Very Revd Frederick W. Dwelly, first Dean of Liverpool. A congregation of 2,000 attended the funeral service on May 13th which was conducted by Bishop Martin. His ashes were initially laid to rest in the sanctuary. In 1961 the casket was moved to rest behind his memorial situated in the South Choir aisle. He also features in the *Scholars'* window.

In June to celebrate 750 years since the granting of Liverpool's Charter (in 1207 King John granted Letters Patent and in 1229 his son Henry III gave Liverpool a Charter constituting a free borough) a series of services were held in the Cathedral. Queen Elizabeth the Queen Mother visited the Cathedral during a day spent in Liverpool in connection with the Charter celebrations. After viewing the statues of herself and King George VI the Queen Mother listened to a special programme of music by the choir. She then took tea with Dean Dillistone and Mrs. Dillistone.

On Sunday October 27th a Memorial was unveiled in the South arm of the East Transept to Admiral Sir Max Horton (1883/1951), Commander-in-Chief Western Approaches. The sermon was given by the Revd O. R. Fulljames, R.N.V.R Naval Chaplain on Merseyside to Western Approaches Command. The memorial is composed of a horizontal panel at the base, surmounted by a smaller upright panel in the centre, in which is carved a mourning Britannia seated in a chair at the sea's edge. She holds in one hand a trident as Mistress of the sea and in the other offers a wreath of victory. At the base of the panel is a sport of dolphins. HMS Dolphin was the Royal Navy shore establishment sited at Fort Blockhouse in Gosport, and was the home of the Royal Navy Submarine Service from 1904 to 1999. The panel is surmounted by a gilt naval crown from depends festoons flanking the Westmorland green slate frame. This joins the mouldings of the major marble panel in the centre.

At either end of these mouldings are gilt flames suggesting eternal vigilance. In the centre of the top mouldings is a plaque in gold and enamels of the pendant of the Order of Bath, of which Sir Max Horton was 'King at Arms'. Also in gold and enamel are the seal of the 'Order' on the left, and the badge of the 'Order' on the right of the central panel. The badge of the 'Order' carries the inscription bearing the name of Sir Max Horton and a very brief record of the many honours that were conferred upon him. On the left is a shortened version of the eulogy expressed by Dean Dwelly at his funeral in 1951. On the right is an extract from the Admiralty report of his activities as Commander-in-Chief Western Approaches. The memorial was designed and executed by Edward Carter Preston.

## 1958

In May the death occurred of Bishop Gresford Jones (1870/1958). He commenced his ministry in Liverpool in 1898 and served as Suffragan Bishop of Warrington from 1927 to 1946.

In August the death of Mr. H.M. Alderson Smith was announced. He was a member of the Executive Committee from 1919 and acted as Chapter clerk.

On October 3rd Miss Christine Wagstaff secretary to Dean Dwelly died. The resting place of her ashes is to be found near the memorial to Dean Dwelly. There is an inscribed stone, carved by Edward Carter Preston, in the pavement of the South Choir aisle.

In October Dean Dillistone reported that, since the beginning of the year, 250 organized parties, representing a total of 15,000 people had conducted tours around the Cathedral.

Mr. Harry James, father of the Clerk of works, who had served as a master mason on the site for 36 years died in November.

The Lady Chapel was re-pointed.

The Cathedral organ was cleaned and overhauled. The Choir console was electrified.

The Western Rooms were opened for public meetings and the British Council of Churches held the first assembly in the rooms.

Mr. Ronald Woan formed the Cathedral Singers.

Mr. Thomas Morgan was appointed Chapter Clerk.

Mr. R. Helsby retired after 28 years at Church House. He acted as General Secretary of the Cathedral Committee for twenty five years.

# 1960

*Sir Giles Gilbert Scott died on February 9th in his 80th year at University College Hospital, London. After a Requiem Mass at St James', Spanish Place, London, a Service of Commemoration and Thanksgiving was held in the Cathedral on February 22nd.*

*The ship's bell of the cruiser HMS Liverpool. The bell is rung daily at midday for a time of prayer.*

As a result of the generosity of Dr. Francis Neilson the lighting of the Choir and Reredos was improved. Bronze hand rails were fixed on the left side of the Rankin porch.

## 1959

On May 3rd the ship's bell of the cruiser HMS *Liverpool* was presented to the Cathedral by Admiral Sir Richard Onslow (1904/1975) on behalf of the Western Approaches Command. During the Second World War HMS *Liverpool* served in the Far East, the Mediterranean and in the Home Fleet. The bell was originally fixed to the wall of the gatehouse at the entrance to Tobruk War Cemetery.

On Sunday September 13th the service of Holy Communion was televised by A.B.C. Television.

The tower was floodlit from December 6th for one month to celebrate the 'Jubilee' of the Institute of Illuminating Engineers.

A Thanksgiving Service, to mark the laying up of 'Colours' by the King's Liverpool Regiment, was held in the Cathedral. The Regiment was amalgamated with the former Manchester Regiment to form the King's Regiment (Manchester and Liverpool). The colours flank the stone case in which is lodged the remembrance book recording the names of the 950 who lost their lives in Second World War. Contained in the niche above the stone case is a book of remembrance for those who have lost their life since the Second World War.

The inscription; 'This Porch was named Welsford, in memory of James Hughes Welsford, ship owner of Liverpool 1863-1917', was carved at the exterior entrance to the North porch.

The Eastern end of the Choir, and the Triforium balustrade were re-pointed. The flat asphalt roofs of the Choir aisle annexes were replaced with copper.

## 1960

The death occurred on January 19th of Canon Lionel Jacob (1893/1960), the Cathedral 'Guest Master'. An inscribed stone in the pavement of the South Choir aisle indicates where his ashes rest.

Sir Giles Gilbert Scott died on February 9th in his 80th year at University College Hospital, London. After a Requiem Mass at St James', Spanish Place, London, a Service of Commemoration and Thanksgiving was held in the Cathedral on February 22nd. He was buried by the Benedictine Monks of Ampleforth in a grave situated outside the Cathedral.

In February, The 'Cathedral Builders' became 'The Friends and Builders of Liverpool Cathedral'. As a result, help for maintenance as well as for the building fund was established. With the completion of the building of the Cathedral in 1978 the title was changed to 'The Friends of Liverpool Cathedral'.

The reconditioning of the Cathedral organ, begun in 1958, was completed. It included the installation of a humidifying plant.

Mr. H.V. James, the Clerk of Works resigned.

On October 3rd a televised service was held to mark the 20th anniversary of the 'Battle of Britain'.

At the Morning Service, on Sunday December 11th, Lord Derby unveiled the Memorial to Dean Frederick W. Dwelly. The life sized bas relief of the Dean, with accompanying figures representing the Cross Guild which he founded, is carved in Ancaster stone from Lincolnshire. The memorial was designed by Edward Carter Preston and the sculptor's final work in the Cathedral. A casket containing the Dean's ashes lies behind the memorial. A Thanksgiving Service for the life and work of Dean Dwelly was held in the afternoon.

The Christmas Day Festival and Eucharist was televised by the A.B.C. Television Company.

Dean Dillistone's *The Pictorial History of Liverpool Cathedral* was published.

Work began on carving the twenty four arms of the English Dioceses, which had been created since 1904, on the shields found in the spandrels of the Nave aisle arches.

The Revd Laurence A. Brown (1907/1994) was consecrated the 5th Suffragan Bishop of Warrington. He served until 1969 when he became Bishop of Birmingham.

A new embroidery circle was formed to help with repairs and replacements. Miss Dorothy Spittle headed the team of ladies.

## 1961

In April the first Bay of the Nave was completed. The Nave Arch (now referred to as the Dulverton Bridge) was completed. The Trustees of the Dulverton Trust donated £44,577 to the cost of the Arch. The wood work was executed in oak by Morrison & Sons with the assistance of Graves and Groves of London who did the carving. Much of the stonework was by Mr. John Rowbottom, Master Mason, who commenced working on the site in 1932. John retired in 1981 after 49 years devoted service to the Cathedral. His brother Tom also served his apprenticeship at the Cathedral. Their Grandfather James, who died in the First World War, was employed on the Lady Chapel from 1906 to 1914.

# 1961

*In April the first Bay of the Nave was completed. The Nave Arch (now referred to as the Dulverton Bridge) was completed. The final cost of the Arch was £44,577.*

Dr. Francis Neilson (1866/1961) a generous donor to the Building Fund, died on April 13th in New York. His funeral service was held in the Cathedral on April 18th. His ashes were interred in the South Nave aisle. A portrait in oil by the American artist Leopold Seyffert (1887/1956) hangs outside the Neilson room.

On Saturday April 22nd Sir Alan Tod, Chairman of the Cathedral Committee opened the First Bay of the Nave which was dedicated by Bishop Martin.

At a Thanksgiving Service on May 7th Coastal Command R.A.F. presented a chalice and paten of silver gilt in memory of the airmen who gave their lives in the Battle of the Atlantic. An inscribed memorial stone was placed in the War Memorial Chapel by the North West Royal Air Forces Association dedicated to those who served in the Royal Air Force.

On May 31st The Most Revd Michael Ramsey was appointed the 100th Archbishop of Canterbury (1904/1988). Archbishop Michael was ordained in 1928 and was curate at Our Lady and St Nicholas Church, Liverpool, for two years. During his ministry in Liverpool he was influenced by the distinguished theologian the Revd Charles Raven, Canon at Liverpool Cathedral.

Mr. A. E. Allen was appointed Clerk of Works.

Sir Alan Tod after 27 years as Chairman of the Cathedral Committee resigned. He was appointed President of the Cathedral, a post which had been vacant since 1953. Sir Alan was succeeded by Lt-Colonel James Malcolm Harrison.

Mr. Philip Radcliffe Evans, grandson of Sir Frederick

Radcliffe, was appointed with Mr. Bromfield, joint treasurer of the Executive Committee. Mr. Evans, with Sir Radcliffe's daughters Mrs. Watson and Mrs. Denman generously contributed towards the printing of the Radcliffe Collection catalogue held at Liverpool Hope University.

Colonel Vere Cotton retired from the Honorary Secretaryship of the Executive Committee. He was succeeded by his son Simon Cotton.

Miss Kathleen Bickersteth, the first secretary of 'Cathedral Builders' died.

It was necessary to re-roof the Eastern Vestries and re-point the Choir and Chapter House. The oak beams of the vestry roofs were replaced with concrete and the asphalt with copper. The interior ceilings remained unaltered.

## 1962

In November the French composer Hector Berlioz's (1803/1869) *Grand Messe des Morts* (Requiem) was performed in the Cathedral. With the completion of the first Bay of the Nave the choir and orchestra were sited at the West end of the Cathedral.

Bishop Christopher Chavasse (1884/1962) son of Bishop Chavasse of Liverpool died in March.

The Revd Henry Ellis, who had served in the Diocese since his ordination in 1932, was appointed Canon Precentor. Canon Ellis was previously Vicar of Prescot.

Mr. George G. Pace was appointed consultant architect. The Corinthian Lodge of the Order of Women

*The Dulverton Bridge, the gift of the Dulverton Trustees. The Dulverton Trust which is an independant charitable grant making organisation, was established in 1949 by the 1st Lord Dulverton.*

Photo: © Gerry Simons

# 1963

*January marked the B.B.C's first television programme from the Cathedral when the Epiphany Service was broadcast.*

*Epstein's sculpture; Liverpool Resurgent.*

Freemasons presented a green frontal for the Lady Chapel. The frontal was designed by Mr. George Pace and executed by Miss Spittle.

Permission was given to the Ordnance Survey to site a triangulation station on the roof of the Cathedral.

## 1963

January marked the B.B.C's first television programme from the Cathedral when the Epiphany Service was broadcast.

Due to the harsh weather conditions work on the Cathedral was shut down in January and February.

Dean Dillistone resigned. Amongst his personal innovations was the periodic choral celebrations of Holy Communion in place of Matins and the broadcasting and televising of services. Dean Dillistone died in 1993 at the age of 90. His name is engraved on the paving at the entrance to the Choir where his ashes rest. His name is also incised into the South Choir aisle wall near to the 'Bishop's Gate'.

Mr. Tom Stone, who had served on the Executive Committee for forty two years, died.

The Executive Committee decided that construction of the third, and last, Bay of the Nave, should be started.

## 1964

The Revd Edward H. Patey, a Residentiary Canon of Coventry Cathedral, was installed the third Dean of Liverpool on May 16th.

On July 6th Mr. Walter Henry Goss-Custard died at the age of 93. He was the first Cathedral organist and President of Liverpool District Organists and Choirmasters Association. He was the Cathedral organist from 1917 to 1955. It was to him more than to any other individual can be attributed the establishment of the Cathedral's musical reputation. His memorial is to be found in the North Choir aisle. His portrait and that of his great uncle Sir John Goss (1800/1880) appears in the *Musicians'* window.

In July the death occurred of Canon F.A. Redwood who was Canon Residentiary and Guest Master from 1960. Before his appointment he was vicar of Ormskirk for 28 years. He was succeeded, as Guest-Master, by the Revd E. Nickson, a Diocesan Canon and former Vicar of St. Cyprian's, Edgehill.

Col. Vere Cotton's *Book of Liverpool Cathedral* was published.

A week of celebrations on the 60th Anniversary of the laying of the Foundation Stone by King Edward VII was held. The celebrations included Mahler's great symphony conducted by Charles Groves (later Sir) and a Diocesan Choirs Festival. On Sir Charles' death in 1992 a Thanksgiving Service was held in the Cathedral.

Canon Charles Raven (1884/1964) died on July 8th at his Cambridge home. He was a renowned orator and established an informal evening service each Sunday in the Cathedral which drew large congregations.

The Revd Gordon Bates was appointed the first full time Diocesan Youth Chaplain and a Chaplain of the Cathedral.

An inscription, recording the donor of the Nave Arch, was carved near the foot of the stair-case on the North side of the arch. It reads, ' A Gift From The Dulverton Trust Made Possible The Building Of This Nave Arch MCMLXI'.

During the summer, Jacob Epstein's (1880/1959) sculpture's *Genesis* (depiction of maternity) and *Jacob and the Angel* (Genesis Chap 32 v 24-32) were exhibited in the corridor of the Western Rooms. Epstein's sculpture *Liverpool Resurgent* (statue of a nude man), which is above the main entrance to the now closed Lewis's store, is well known to the people of Liverpool.

Mr. George Hughes who was for twelve years a part-time verger and in charge of the bookstall died.

The Chapter architect Mr.George Pace designed a Holy Table (which recalls a carpenters bench) credence tables, and houseling benches in oak with a standing cross and candlesticks in wrought iron for use when Holy Communion is celebrated in the Central Space. The Holy Table, in memory of Robert Coltart and Edith Battersby his wife and also Alan Herbert, was the gift of their daughter. Another example of George Pace's work is to be found at All Saints Church, Childwall where in 1971 he designed an oak communion table in memory of the Revd Ronald Hunter who served as vicar from 1925 to 1948.

## 1965

On January 30th the Cathedral's bourdon bell, Great George, was tolled by Messrs Bell, Mitchel and Williams, to mark the state funeral of Sir Winston Churchill (1874/1965), which took place at St Paul's Cathedral, London.

In March the death occurred of Mr. E. R. Bickersteth-Earnshaw, a member of the Executive Committee from 1952.

On March 2nd the death occurred of the Liverpool

# 1965

*On March 2nd the death occurred of the Liverpool born sculptor and artist Edward Carter Preston (1885/1965).*

*Bishop Blanch, the 5th Bishop of Liverpool.*

born sculptor and artist Edward Carter Preston (1885/1965). During a thirty year period of work in the Cathedral he produced fifty sculptures, ten memorials and several reliefs. As a medalist he produced the memorial plaque that was presented to the next of kin of all who died in, or as a result of, the First World War. His youngest daughter Julia (1926/2011) also an artist and potter, who specialised in *sgraffito* decoration on plates and ceramics, modelled with other family members for a number of his carvings. Julia was responsible for the decorative bowl used for the baptisms that take place in the Lady Chapel.

Bishop Martin retired on November 30th. To mark his retirement over two thousand people attended a service in the Cathedral. He proclaimed 'you have to go to Liverpool Cathedral if you want to see how to walk to the glory of God. Every procession is an act of worship'. During his episcopate he oversaw the diocesan programme of the re-building of churches damaged during the war. As a result he had a close relationship with the parishes of the Diocese, who came to look upon the Cathedral as 'the mother Church of the Diocese' in fact, as well as theory. On his retirement he was appointed Honorary Fellow of St Peter's, Oxford.

On December 22nd it was announced that Canon Stuart Yarworth Blanch, Canon Residentiary of Rochester Cathedral and Warden of Rochester Theological College had been appointed 5th Bishop of Liverpool.

The Dean and Chapter petitioned against a Liverpool Corporation Bill to build two motorway-type roads on the two sides of St James's Mount.

Mr. J.H. Bromfield resigned as Joint Honorary Treasurer, a position he had held from 1946.

Lady Harvey, in memory of her parents Richard Robertson Lockett (1846/1905) and Isabella Maria Lockett (1849/1944), presented a two manual recital console. Built on a mobile platform, with sixty feet of spare cable, it enabled the organist to play the main organ either from the Memorial Chapel, the Central Space or near to the Choir. Carved on the rear of the console is the family crest which bears the family motto 'non nobis solum' (not for ourselves alone).

The sculpture, *The Holy Family*, was presented to the Cathedral. It was sculpted by Josefina de Vasconcellos (1904/2005). Josefina lived with her husband Delmar Banner, the artist and Anglican lay preacher, at The Beld in Little Langdale, Cumbria. The sculpture is said to have the shape of Langdale Pike which she could see from the window of her home. Gloucester Cathedral has an almost identical work.

Mr. Jack Kitchings retired as Cathedral Foreman. He was succeeded by Mr. Alan Stone.

The Church Assembly passed the *Prayer Book* (alternative and other services) measure.

Rupert Hoare was ordained priest in the Cathedral. Thirty five years later The Rt Revd Hoare was installed as the 5th Dean of Liverpool and served from 2000 to 2007.

The Crofters, a folk group, was formed. Its four members were, Dave Johnston, John Poole, Phil Duncalf and Steve Clarke. The first three were members of the Cross Guild.

# 1966

At York Minster on March 25th, the Feast of the Annunciation, Canon Stuart Yarworth Blanch was consecrated Bishop of Liverpool by Archbishop Coggan of York.

On Monday April 25th, St Mark's Day, Bishop Blanch was enthroned in the Cathedral.

On May 1st a Service of Thanksgiving for the life of Sir Frederick Lister (1867/1966), the co-founder and the first Chairman of the British Legion, was held in the Cathedral.

The poet laureate Sir John Betjeman (1906/1982), broadcast the immortal words, when describing the interior of the Cathedral, 'Suddenly one sees; that the greatest art of architecture that lifts one up and turns one into a king, yet compels reverence, is the art of enclosing space'.

On October 3rd and 4th the Liverpool Everyman Theatre presented two performances in the Lady Chapel of the poet Christopher Fry's *A Sleep of Prisoners,* an anti-war verse drama in the form of a modern passion play.

On October 31st and November 1st the English Opera Group gave the first performance in the North of England of Benjamin Britten's opera for Church presentation *The Burning Fiery Furnace*. The work tells the story of Nebuchadnezzar and the three Israelites, Ananias, Misael and Asarias (Shadrach, Meschach and Abednego) who were thrown into a furnace for their refusal to worship Nebuchadnezzar's image of gold. However, God saved them from death as the voice of an angel joins the Israelites in a '*Benedicite*'. The story is portrayed by Carl Edwards in the Cathedral's *Benedicite* window.

Mr. Reginald Clucas, who had worked many hours on the difficult acoustic problems of the Cathedral, died after a long illness.

# 1967

*In April, for the first time, a Roman Catholic cleric preached in the Cathedral when Bishop Augustine Harris gave the address at the United Voluntary Organisation Service.*

The temporary wall between the First and the Second Bay of the Nave was demolished.

The death occurred of Mr. Robert Helsby, Secretary to the Cathedral Committee from 1933 to 1958.

Mr. Ernest Pratt was appointed Deputy Organist.

The Renaissance Music Group was formed. The choir specialises in European Choral music composed up to the middle of the 17th century. The choir performs two concerts each year in the Lady Chapel of the Cathedral.

Mr. J. C. Macgregor was appointed Cathedral bursar. He succeeded Mr. Trevor Entwistle.

A Thanksgiving Service was held in the Cathedral to celebrate the centenary of the founding of Dr Barnardos. The first Barnardos home in Liverpool, 'The Ever Open Door', was opened in 1892 at 142a Islington. In 1920 the home was moved to 17 Falkner Square, close to the Cathedral.

The Liverpool Churches Ecumenical Council was formed under the Chairmanship of Dean Patey.

## 1967

In February the Morning Service was moved from 11am to 10.30am. After the service coffee was served to the congregation for the first time in the Western Rooms.

In March the firm of Morrison & Sons went into liquidation. Construction continued by direct labour under the auspices of Liverpool Cathedral Contractors Ltd.

On April 13th the adoption of a new design for the West front of the Cathedral was announced. In this design, much of the 1942 plan went, there was to be no Narthex, no internal Gallery and no *Porte Cochère*. The alterations to Scott's design allowed for the inclusion of the West Window. The design was by the architect Mr. Frederick G.S. Thomas (1898/1984), the partner and office manager to Sir Giles. He was assisted by the architect Mr. Roger Arthur Philip Pinckney (1900/1990) who had also worked with Sir Giles.

Canon James S. Bezzant (1897/1967), a notable theologian and brilliant preacher, and who was Canon Residentiary and Chancellor of the Cathedral from 1932 to 1952, died on March 27th. A Memorial Service was held on Saturday April 22nd.

In April, for the first time, a Roman Catholic cleric preached in the Cathedral when Bishop Augustine Harris gave the address at the United Voluntary Organisation Service.

On May 10th a conference entitled 'Women in Holy Orders' took place in the Cathedral.

On Whit Sunday May 14th the Metropolitan Cathedral was consecrated. The Cathedral was designed by Sir Frederick Gibberd (1908/1984), architect, town planner and landscape designer. Construction of Gibberd's design began in 1962 following the abortion of Adrian Gilbert Scott's (1882/1963) commission in 1953 to work on a smaller version of Lutyens' design.

In July four Cross Guild boys broke the world record by playing table tennis continuously for 126 hours and 1 minute. The financial proceeds went to Christian Aid.

*Drawing illustrating the original plan for the West End of the Cathedral.*

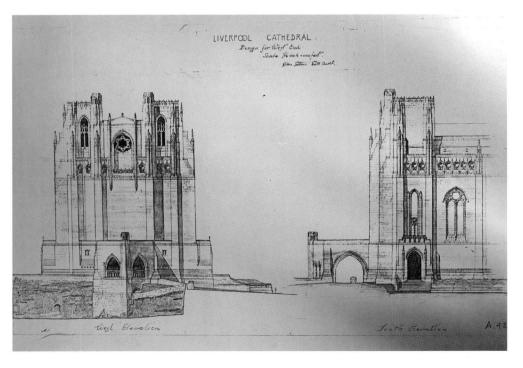

# 1968

*On May 5th a service of 'Thanksgiving for Victory in the Battle of the Atlantic' was televised by the B.B.C. Amongst those present was Admiral of the Fleet, Earl Mountbatten (1900/1979).*

*Statue of Henry Cotton, Chairman of the Cathedral Executive Committee and first Chancellor of Liverpool John Moores University. The statue, sculpted by Tom Murphy, is situated outside the Henry Cotton building.*

The creation of a new administrative organisation rendered the post of Clerk of Works, occupied by Mr. Allen, redundant. Mr. James R. Bambridge was appointed Contract Manager.

Mr. Simon Cotton, Honorary Secretary of the Executive Committee from 1961, resigned. He was succeeded by Mr. E. Rowland Ball. The Cotton family connection, with the work of the Cathedral, continued and in 1979 Simon's brother Henry Cotton (1929/1993), who had been a member of the committee from 1973, was appointed Chairman of the Executive Committee. During his period in office he played a major role in supervising the details of the arrangements for the completion of the Cathedral. A memorial plaque to him is situated in the North Choir aisle. Henry was the first Chancellor of Liverpool John Moores University and a statue of him is situated outside the Henry Cotton Building. Dame Elizabeth Frink's 14ft bronze statue *The Welcoming Christ* over the exterior of the West door was the gift of Mrs. Susan Cotton in memory of her husband Henry.

On November 28th Her Royal Highness Princess Margaret visited the Cathedral.

Mr. Owen Pittaway, who for thirty two years was Clerk of Works, died. He was involved in the work of the Cathedral for a total of 46 years. In 1920 he was appointed Assistant Clerk of Works and succeeded Mr. A. Green a year later as Clerk of Works.

As part of the Cathedral's Christmas festive programme the televised Christmas Eve Service 'How On Earth' included a performance by the singing group 'The Bee Gees'. Passages of the Bible were read, 'in Scouse', by Kenny Everett (1944/1995), the radio D.J. and television entertainer.

Girls from St Edmunds College, Liverpool performed a dance interpretation of the Passion against the dramatic backcloth of the *Te Deum* window.

A boxing ring was put up in the Central Space for a service entitled *Gloves off for Nigeria*. The boxers symbolised the fight against ignorance, poverty and disease in the Third World. The service was organised by the Church Missionary Society,

The American Everyman Players performed a dramatic interpretation of the Epistle to the Romans.

Bishop Blanch gave a series of lectures in the Cathedral entitled *Faith in a Space Age*. (On July 21st 1969 Neil Armstrong was the first person to walk on the moon).

## 1968

Sir Charles A. Gladstone (1888/1968), a member of

the Executive Committee from 1947 to 1964 died on April 22nd. Sir Charles, a master at Eton College, was the grandson of William Ewart Gladstone.

The Second Bay of the Nave was dedicated on May 4th by Bishop Blanch. To mark the occasion Archbishop Coggan of York preached at the service.

Woolston, a form of polyester resin reinforced with fibre glass and faced with a surface coating of resin and sand, was used for the vaulting of the second and third Bays of the Nave.

On May 5th a service of 'Thanksgiving for Victory in the Battle of the Atlantic' was televised by the B.B.C. Amongst those present was Admiral of the Fleet, Earl Mountbatten (1900/1979).

On May 6th a meeting at Liverpool Town Hall was held to launch the £500,000 'Finish the Cathedral' appeal.

Dame Peggy Ashcroft appeared in the Cathedral on Sunday May 19th with the 'Apollo Society' in a programme of poetry and music. Dame Peggy, who at this time was President of the Liverpool Everyman, read the poetry of T. S. Eliot .

During May and June a series of sermons were preached on the lives of some of the clergymen portrayed in the *Parsons'* window, which is situated on the South side of the second Bay of the Nave. Twenty two clerics are portrayed in the window amongst them; William Carlile (1847/1942) who founded the Church Army in 1882 and John Venn (1759/1813) who with Charles Simeon (1759/1836) founded the Church Missionary Society. The left lancet of the window is in memory of William Burton Eills (1857/1936), a Liverpool provision merchant, and his wife Mary Louisa Eills (1855/1934). The family lived at Aigburth Drive, Liverpool. The right lancet is in memory of John Naylor (1856/1906), a private banker, and his wife Magdalene Naylor (1861/1928).

A stone balustrade was added to the Ambo.

The death occurred of the Revd William Vernon Walmsley (1886/1968) Assistant Chaplain at the Cathedral from 1932 to 1949. He was a member of the College of Interpreters, the School of Cantors and the College of Marshalls at the Cathedral.

The new Order of Holy Communion was introduced for a period of four years. This led to the publication of the *Alternative Service Book* (1980) the first complete prayer book produced by the Church of England since 1662. This in turn was succeeded by the *Book of Common Worship* in 1998.

An exhibition, depicting the life and story of the

# 1969

*On January 1st Deaconess Thelma Tomlinson joined the Cathedral staff as a Chaplain. At this time women were restricted to the role of parish worker or deaconess.*

Photo: © Geoff Shipley

*The Cricketers' Chair*

Benedictine community was mounted by a Benedictine monk from Ampleforth

Dean Patey was appointed Vice-Chairman of the Council of B.B.C. Radio Merseyside. He worked alongside the Revd Jim Pollard the religious service producer of Radio Merseyside. In 1980 the Revd Pollard presented the gift of a President's Chair ('the Cricketers' Chair') in memory of his wife Rita.

The Memorial to Dr. H. Goss Custard was dedicated prior to the annual anniversary organ recital. The memorial is situated in the North Choir aisle. Behind it are immured his ashes, and those of his wife.

## 1969

On January 1st Deaconess Thelma Tomlinson joined the Cathedral staff as a Chaplain. At this time women were restricted to the role of parish worker or deaconess. In 1975 she was appointed Diocesan Advisor for Lay Ministry. Deaconess Thelma who retired in 1981 was the first woman minister on the staff of an English Cathedral to undertake a full ministry of preaching, leading worship and pastoral work. On the 14th June 1987 seventeen women were deaconed in the Cathedral and took on full responsibility as Deacons. Seven years later Bishop David Sheppard ordained 26 women to be priests. Amongst those ordained was the Revd Cynthia Dowdle who in 2008 was appointed the first woman Residentiary Canon of the Cathedral.

The 'Cathedral Builders' 44th Anniversary Service took place on Saturday 31st May. The preacher was the Rt Revd Charles Claxton, Bishop of Blackburn and former Bishop of Warrington. In the evening Donald Swann (1923/1994), of the Flanders-Swann 'At The Drop of a Hat' team, performed in the Cathedral.

On June 1st a Thanksgiving Service was held in the Cathedral to mark the 125th anniversary of the founding of the Y.M.C.A. The Association, which was founded in London in 1844 by Sir George Williams (1821/1905), was first established in Liverpool in 1846.

Bishop Trevor Huddleston visited the Cathedral on July 13th and presented a lecture entitled *The Future of Africa.*

All the masons engaged on the site came out on strike on August 29th.

On October 16th a recital by Yehudi Menuhin (1916/1999) in aid of the 'Appeal Fund' was held in the Cathedral. Yehudi Menuhin, who was born in New York, is considered to be one of the greatest violinists of the 20 century. The concert raised £700 which was divided between the Yehudi Menuhin School and the Appeal Fund.

As a result of the Synodical Government measure the Church Assembly renamed and reconstituted itself as the General Synod of the Church of England.

The Eucharist became the principle service on a Sunday.

Mr. Ted Hall succeeded Mr. Jim Davies as Head Verger.

The Western Rooms were re-decorated and a new lighting system installed.

The first sandstone from St. Bees was delivered. The cliff side quarry is situated on the coast at Salton Bay, St Bees Head, south of Whitehaven, Cumbria. The quarry has been worked since medieval times and the red sandstone was an ideal match for the Woolton stone.

Mr. Alan Stone the General Foreman retired. He began work at the Cathedral in 1934 as a banker mason and, after military service in the Second World War, returned to the Cathedral in 1953 as foreman mason.

A portrait of Dr. Francis Neilson, by Leopold Seyffert (1887/1956) the American artist, was presented to the Cathedral.

An exhibition of photographs assembled by the Imperial War Graves Commission were shown in the War Memorial Chapel.

Miss Mary Moore of Chicago donated £500 to pay for a vestry door in the second Bay of the Nave in memory of her mother Mrs. Sabina Hind Moore who was born in Liverpool. Miss Moore also paid for the adjoining door in memory of her aunt Mary Sophia Hind.

The Dean of St Paul's Cathedral, Namirembe, Kampala, The Very Revd Yokana Mukasa, was a guest of the Cathedral Chapter, sharing in their day-to-day activities.

## 1970

In January a Unity service during the Week of Prayer provoked noisy protests.

The Cathedral site re-opened on Monday February 20th after the masons' strike.

On February 1st the Revd John Lawton, Vicar of Kirkby, was installed Archdeacon of Warrington. He succeeded the Revd Eric Evans who retired after ten years of service as Archdeacon. The Revd Evans was appointed Archdeacon *Emiritus.*

On February 20th the Revd Gordon Bates, who during his ministry in the Cathedral, held the position of Diocesan Youth Chaplain, Precentor and Director of Ordinands, was installed Vicar of Huyton. Amongst his ordinands was the Revd Myles Davies who was

# 1970

*A production of 'Noyes Fludde', Benjamin Britten's musical setting of the medieval version of the Noah story was performed in the Cathedral at the end of April.*

*The Revd Myles Davies who was appointed Canon Residentiary in 2006 and Canon Chancellor in 2008.*

appointed Canon Residentiary in 2006 and Canon Precentor in 2008. The Revd Bates was succeeded by the Revd Alan Ripley as Diocesan Youth Chaplain and Cathedral Chaplain. In 1975 Bishop Sheppard appointed the Revd Ripley as his personal Chaplain.

In the Cathedral on April 7th Canon John Bickersteth was Consecrated the 6th Suffragan Bishop of Warrington by Archbishop Coggan of York . The occasion was marked by the use of the newly published Liturgical Commission's draft Ordinal. The first major re-ordering of the service for consecrating bishops since the publication of the Book of Common Prayer in 1662. Interestingly at this date the newly formed General Synod had not considered the new Ordinal. Bishop Bickersteth is a member of the family of Bickersteth whose name is recorded in the *Scholars'* window.

A production of *Noyes Fludde*, Benjamin Britten's musical setting of the medieval version of the Noah story was performed in the Cathedral at the end of April.

On May 2nd a Thanksgiving Service to celebrate the Diamond Jubilee of the Girl Guides Association was held in the Cathedral. The Girl Guides was formed in 1910 by Robert Baden-Powell (1857/1941) with the help of his sister Agnes. After his marriage in 1912 his wife Olave took a major role in the development of girl guiding and girl scouting. Olave died in 1977 and a Thanksgiving Service was held in the Cathedral to thank God for her life and work.

To mark the 350th Anniversary of Merchant Taylors School, Crosby, Archbishop Coggan of York preached at a Thanksgiving Service on May 15th. The school was founded in 1620 by John Harrison, a Merchant Taylor of London, who was born in Great Crosby. On May 22nd a 'Centenary Service' was held for the Sisters of the Church, the Anglican Women's Religious Order. The Order was founded in 1870 by Mother Emily Ayckbown.

On June 28th a Thanksgiving Service to celebrate the centenary of the founding of the British Red Cross Society was held in the Cathedral. The society was founded in August 1870 following the establishment in 1863 by Henry Dunant (1828/1910) of the International Red Cross and Red Crescent movement.

As part of the 'Finish the Cathedral' appeal, a flower festival was held in June. It was recorded that over 40,000 people came to the festival. Included in the magnificent floral displays was a 30ft Cross, which contained over 6,000 carnations. The exhibits were arranged by Mrs. Margaret Hewitt of Hightown, Mrs. Mary Allen of Ormskirk, and the members of the Flower Arrangement Association of the North West.

The festival raised over £4,000 for the 'Appeal Fund'. The Cathedral welcomed the French boys' choir *Les Petits Chanteurs a la Croix Potence* on their first visit to England. They gave a recital on July 8th.

In July Mr. J.A. Raymond presented to the Dean a Bible and Prayer Book engraved Cathedral *Church of St Peter-the-Pro-Cathedral*. Mr. Raymond's father, to whom the book belonged, was the last presiding organist at St Peter's.

Mr. Harry Brooks (1909/ 1970), Chief Steward for ten years, died on July 15th. His funeral service was held in the Cathedral. He was succeeded by Mr. Ernest Hambleton.

In August, an exhibition of the life and works of the German composer and pianist, Ludwig Van Beethoven (1770/1827), was held in the Cathedral. The exhibition attracted over 15,000 visitors.

On September 7th Sir Alan Cecil Tod (1887/1970) President of the Cathedral Committee died. A 'Thanksgiving Service' for the life and work of Sir Alan was held on September 15th. In 1954, when receiving from Liverpool University the Honorary Degree of Doctor of Law, he was thus described 'in the world of commerce (insurance, banking, shipping and cotton) he is a colossus'. His ashes lie in the South Nave aisle where his name is inscribed on the floor. A memorial stone to Sir Alan is placed in the North East Choir aisle. The *Benedicite* window was the gift of Sir Alan and his wife Dame Helen who were both generous benefactors of the Cathedral. The left lancet of the *Laymen's* window is also to Sir Alan's memory. The right lancet of the *Bishops'* window is in memory of his parents Archibald (1851/1927) an East Indian merchant and Alice (1858/1946).

Mr. Brian Runnett, organist of Norwich Cathedral, and an assistant organist at the Cathedral from 1965 to 1967 died in a car accident on August 20th. His funeral service was held at Holy Trinity Church, Southport.

On September 13th The North West Region Air Training Corps presented the propeller of a Pusher Biplane Fighter. The plane was used as a fighter in the First World War from August 1916.

In November Synodical Government was inaugurated.

On November 19th the death occurred of Colonel Vere Egerton Cotton (1888/1970). He was a member of the Executive Committee from 1922 and author of *The Book of Liverpool Cathedral*. A Memorial Service was held in the Cathedral on December 1st. The address was given by Sir James Mountford. A memorial to Colonel Cotton was fixed in the wall of the last bay, on the South side of the Cathedral. Mr.

# 1971

*On January 8th Lord Caccia (1905/1990) the British diplomat and Lord Prior of the Most Venerable Order of the Hospital of St John of Jerusalem presided at a ceremony in the Cathedral during which twenty ambulance cadets, and twenty nursing cadets were enrolled.*

*Sir Giles Gilbert Scott and Lady Louise Scott's gravestone, situated outside the Cathedral.*

*Memorial stone to Sir Giles Gilbert Scott set into the paving of the Central Space.*

*Photos: © Gerry Simons*

C.F. J. Beausire succeeded Colonel Cotton as Chairman of the Stained Glass Committee.

Mrs. Bessie Brooks reported, that with her helpers, over 25,000 cups of tea and coffee were served during the year in the Western Rooms.

All stocks of Woolton Quarry stone were exhausted.

Mr. John Turton, together with his brothers and sisters, gave £7,000 to pay for the Great West Door. Mr. Turton was a director of the builders Morrison and Sons Ltd. His name is inscribed on the doors and is also remembered as one of the firm's directors on the Cathedral's third bell, which is named *Chad*.

## 1971

On January 8th Lord Caccia (1905/1990) the British diplomat and Lord Prior of the Most Venerable Order of the Hospital of St John of Jerusalem presided at a ceremony in the Cathedral during which twenty ambulance cadets, and twenty nursing cadets were enrolled.

On February 12th, three days before the halfpenny ceased to be legal tender, a group of four and five year olds from the Primary department of St David's Sunday School, Childwall, presented to the Dean 11,081 halfpennies (£23) for the 'Finish the Cathedral' Appeal. Other events organised for the 'Appeal' included a South Liverpool midnight marathon (£525), a Garden Party in the Parish of St Michael's, Aughton (£248), and a Farnworth and Widnes sponsored walk (£855).

On April 6th the French playwright Henri Gheon's (1875/1944) play *The Way of the Cross* was presented, by William Fry and Sylvia Read of Theatre Roundabout, in the Nave. The play consists of fourteen short scenes based on the Stations of the Cross.

A Service of Thanksgiving was held in the Cathedral on June 13th to celebrate the British Legion's 'Golden Jubilee'. The Legion presented an Altar cloth in the Legion's colours, blue and gold. The British Legion was formed in May 1921, by Lance Bombardier Tom Lister, as a voice for ex-service personnel. It was in 1921 that the first ever 'Poppy Appeal' was made.

In August the memorial stone to Sir Giles Gilbert Scott was set into the centre of the paving of the Central Space under the Vestey Tower. Mr. Richard Scott, son of Sir Giles, prepared the design based on the 'Catherine wheel' which is incorporated in the Scott family crest.

On October 9th the play *The Just Vengeance* by the detective novelist Dorothy L. Sayer (1893/1957) was held in the Cathedral. The play is a dramatic presentation of the Christian doctrine of the

Atonement and was first perfomed in Lichfield Cathedral in 1946.

On Sunday October 31st Dean Patey preached on the occasion of the Dedication of the South Transept Portal of Washington National Cathedral which stands on St Alban's Mount, high above the United States capital. The building of the Cathedral took place between 1907 and 1990. The Cathedral's first architect was George Frederick Bodley who, before his death, was joint architect with Sir Giles Gilbert Scott in the building of Liverpool Cathedral.

On November 20th Ronald Woan, with the Cathedral Singers and Orchestra, presented Michael Tippett's choral work *A Child of our Time*. A secular oratorio inspired by events in Germany and composed by Michael Tippett (1905/1998) between 1939 and 1941.

A significant addition to the ceremonial of the Holy Communion was introduced with the invitation to members of the congregation to shake hands with their neighbours as a token of Christian brotherhood in the family of Christ.

Mr. Stone, the yard foreman, on his retirement was presented with a gratuity in recognition of his service on the Cathedral site.

The Revd Eric Corbett was installed as Archdeacon of Liverpool. He succeeded the Revd Hubert Wilkinson, who had served as Archdeacon and Vicar of St Mary's, Grassendale for twenty years. Archdeacon Wilkinson commenced his ministry in the Diocese in 1941 as Vicar of Allerton. Canon Corbett resigned his Archdeaconry in 1979 when he succeeded Canon Hopkins as Canon Treasurer. Canon Graham Spiers, Vicar of Aigburth, succeeded Canon Corbett as Archdeacon.

## 1972

The death occurred in January of Mr. Cecil F. J. Beausire, director of the family firm Joseph Beausire & Co and Chairman of the Stained Glass Committee. The right lancet of the *Laymen's* window, situated in the South Nave aisle, is to his memory. He was succeeded by Lord Cozens-Hardy, director of Pilkington Brothers Ltd, St Helens.

Mr. Geoffrey L. Pilkington, who served on the Executive Committee from 1933 to 1951, died in early January.

A letter from Church leaders was read in the Cathedral to launch 'Call to the North'.

In April the Cathedral site was picketed by forty building trade workers demanding the re-instatement of their colleagues previously employed on the site.

# 1973

*The Everyman Theatre's production of T.S.Eliot's (1888/1965) Murder in the Cathedral, a verse drama that portrays the assassination of Archbishop Thomas Beckett, was performed in the Cathedral.*

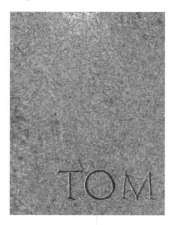

*The memorial paving stone to Tom Douglas.*

*Tom Douglas the Cathedral engineer, who had been employed on the Cathedral site from 1931, when he was 16 years old, retired at the end of November.*

On Whit Sunday May 21st a Thanksgiving Service was held to celebrate the centenary of the Royal Southern Hospital. The hospital closed in 1979.

Canon Henry Hutton Ellis, Precentor of the Cathedral from 1962, died on August 4th. A Thanksgiving Service for his life and ministry was held in the Cathedral on September 23rd. His ministry spanned 40 years in the Diocese, serving in parishes in Wigan, Wavertree and Prescot. His ashes and those of his wife lie in the South Choir aisle.

Mr. Tom Douglas the Cathedral engineer, who had been employed on the Cathedral site from 1931, when he was 16 years old, retired at the end of November. In addition to his role as engineer, when needed, he acted as a verger. After his death, in 1985, his ashes were laid to rest in the Derby transept near to the stairwell leading to the maintenance department. The memorial paving stone bears the simple inscription 'Tom'. He was succeeded in the engineering and maintenance department by Jack Lewington.

The death occurred of Mr. William Wilson (1905/1972) the Scottish stained glass artist, printmaker and water colour painter, who designed the *Bishops'* window. A member of the Royal Scottish Academy, he was described by the University of St Andrews 'as one of Scotland's great artists'. His name appears in the window.

Mr. E. Rowland Ball, Mayor of Crosby from 1970 to 1971, was appointed joint Honorary Secretary of 'Friends and Builders' with Miss Hilary Leather. In 1974 he was appointed the first Mayor of Sefton.

Work commenced on the renovation of the organ in the Lady Chapel.

## 1973

On Sunday January 7th Communion Service (Series 111) was used for the first time in the Cathedral. A setting was composed by John Madden a member of the Cross Guild.

In June the 'Apollo Society' presented a programme of words and music. One of the readers was the actress Janet Suzman.

Nearly one thousand delegates attended The British Council of Churches Youth Conference on August 31st. During the evening and night the Central Space of the Cathedral was transformed into a huge 'fair-ground' where, in various booths were illustrated a wide panorama of concern for the hungry, the under-privileged, the homeless, the illiterate, the persecuted, the prisoner, the alcoholic and drug addict. Dean Patey, in thanking the young people for being present, expressed the view that it

'helped him to see more clearly how the Cathedral might be used'.

Lt. Col. Eric Arden who was the Diocesan Registrar from 1937 to 1973, and who was well known in the Cathedral and the Diocese died in August. His funeral service was held in the Lady Chapel. A vestry door in the North aisle of the Nave was given in his memory. He was succeeded by his son Roger who served as Registrar and Bishop's Legal Secretary in the Liverpool Diocese until 2010. Roger's sister Dame Mary Arden donated a chair for the Lady Chapel in memory of R.H. Arden and Mary Margaret Arden.

Mrs. Sally Pritchard, who for 30 years had served as a Cathedral cleaner, died in August. It was said 'she took special pride in keeping the offices of the Dean and Chancellor clean and tidy'.

Bishop Trevor Huddleston (1913/1998), best known for his anti-apartheid activism and his book *Naught For Your Comfort* (1956), preached in the Cathedral. Nelson Mandela (1918/2013) said of him; 'No white man has done more for South Africa than Trevor Huddleston'.

The Lady Chapel Organ was rebuilt by Messrs Hill, Norman and Beard of London

The Revd Gordon Bates, Vicar of Huyton, was appointed Canon Residentiary and Precentor. In 1983 he was consecrated Bishop of Whitby where he served until 1999.

Canon Leslie Hopkins resigned from the post of Diocesan Director of Education, which he had held from 1962, and became a full member of the Cathedral staff. He had special responsibility for the pastoral care of the Cathedral Company and congregation. He also had general oversight of the Vergers, the Stewards, and the Interpreters. Canon Hopkins retired in 1979.

The Everyman Theatre's production of T.S.Eliot's (1888/1965) *Murder in the Cathedral*, a verse drama that portrays the assassination of Archbishop Thomas Beckett, was performed in the Cathedral. Bishop Blanch and Archbishop Beck were in the audience to watch the first play performed by a repertory company in the Cathedral. The play was first performed in Canterbury Cathedral in 1935.

The 'Friends and Builders' donated a display case to the Cathedral. It is situated by the Chapter House entrance,

The Cathedral organist Noel Rawsthorne appeared on Roy Plomley's radio show *Desert Island Discs.* The show, which was devised by Roy Plomley (1914/1981) in 1941, was first broadcast in January 1942.

# 1974

*Members of choirs from all over Merseyside took part in the television programme 'Songs of Praise' which was recorded in the Cathedral.*

*Mace presented by Sir Douglas Crawford and his sister Jessie.*

## 1974

On March 10th a Thanksgiving Service to mark the 150th anniversary of the Royal National Lifeboat Institution was held in the Cathedral. The institution was established in 1824 by Sir William Hillary (1771/1847) as 'The National Institution for the Preservation of Life from Shipwreck'. It was the North Sunderland lifeboat crew who assisted Grace Darling (1815/1842) and her father as they returned from helping in the rescue of survivors from the shipwrecked SS *Forfarshire*. Grace Darling's portrait appears in the Staircase window.

On April 1, as a result of the Local Government Act of 1972,the County of Merseyside was created. The county comprises the five Metropolitan Boroughs of Knowsley, St Helens, Sefton, Wirral and the City of Liverpool. The first Lord Lieutenant of Merseyside was Sir Douglas Crawford (1904/1981) who held the office until 1979. His name is inscribed, and those of his successors, on the back of a clergy stall on the North side of the Presbytery. In 1980, Sir Douglas and his sister Jessie presented to the Cathedral a mace.

The Commemoration of Victory in the Battle of the Atlantic Service, which took place on Sunday May 5th, was televised.

The annual service, arranged by the local branch of the Royal College of Nursing, in commemoration of the birthday of Florence Nightingale (1820/1910), took place on Sunday, May 12th.

Archbishop Donald Coggan (1909/2000) of York was translated to Canterbury.

On July11th a 'Service of Thanksgiving and the Laying Up of the Colours' of the vessel HMS *Conway* was held in the Cathedral. The vessel *Conway* was a naval training school. Originally stationed on the Mersey during the Second World War it was moved to the Menai Straits. Sadly in 1953 the ship was wrecked when being towed to Birkenhead. The training school moved to Anglesey to purpose built premises. The poet laureate John Masefield (1878/1967), who was a frequent worshipper at the Cathedral, trained on the HMS *Conway* for a life at sea. The sermon was given by The Most Revd Gwilym Williams Archbishop of Wales. The Dean and Chapter received the gift of a fine silver ewer for use at Holy Communion.

On September 11th an 'Inaugural Service' was held in the Cathedral to mark the formation of the Merseyside Churches' Ecumenical Council. The Council replaced the Liverpool Churches' Ecumenical Council.

On November 10th Dr. Martin Niemoller

(1892/1984), a member of the World Council of Churches, and one of the most distinguished Church leaders of the twentieth century, preached at the Annual Service of Remembrance and Reconciliation.

The death occurred in November of Lady Marjorie Tod, the widow of Sir Alan Tod. The funeral service was held in the Lady Chapel on November 13th.

Work began at Delta Metal Rods, Birmingham on the fabrication of the metal for the 15 ton *Benedicite* window. The window is capable of withstanding a high wind load which could reach as much as 50lbs per square foot during exceptional storm conditions. One of the requirements which had to be met was an exposure period of 500 years!

Mr. Ted Hall, after eight years service, retired from his post as Head Verger. He was succeeded by Mr. Len Collins.

At the annual 'Battle of Britain' Service the address was given by Group Captain Leonard Cheshire, V.C (1917/1992), the founder of 'Leonard Cheshire Disability'.

Crown Princess Sonja of Norway visited the Cathedral. Following the death of King Olav in 1991 she became Norway's first Queen Consort in fifty three years.

Mr. C. Holloway who commenced working on the Cathedral in 1935 as a banker mason retired.

Members of choirs from all over Merseyside took part in the television programme *Songs of Praise* which was recorded in the Cathedral.

## 1975

On January 8th a farewell Eucharist, attended by over 2,000 people, was held in the Cathedral for Bishop Blanch before he took up the position of Archbishop of York. Miss Gillian Burrows, a member of the General Synod, made a presentation to the Bishop on behalf of the people of the Diocese of Liverpool. Bishop Blanch was enthroned Archbishop of York on February 25th, when over three hundred people from the Liverpool Diocese travelled to York for the service.

A service was held on May 7th to commemorate the thirtieth anniversary of the 'Liberation of Norway' in 1945. The Service, which was in both in English and Norwegian, was conducted by the Norwegian Pastor of Liverpool and Dean Patey.

On June 4th Canon Hopkins conducted the funeral of Mr. William Christian, a member of the maintenance staff. He joined Morrison's in 1921 at the age of fourteen years and was head joiner when the firm closed in 1967.

# 1975

*The Rt Revd David Sheppard (1929/2005) was installed the sixth Bishop of Liverpool on Wednesday June 11th. Over two thousand people were present in the congregation.*

*The Rt Revd David Sheppard.*

The Rt Revd David Sheppard (1929/2005) was installed the sixth Bishop of Liverpool on Wednesday June 11th. Over two thousand people were present in the congregation. Bishop David had previously served as Bishop of Woolwich from 1969. The BBC *Anno Domini* film relating Bishop David's move to Liverpool was broadcast.

The 'Friends and Builders' Festival Service was held on June 14th. To celebrate the 50th anniversary of the founding of the 'Cathedral Builders' the distinguished preacher the Very Revd Martin Sullivan, Dean of St Paul's, London, addressed the large congregation. Dean Sullivan, who was born in New Zealand, was Dean of St Paul's from 1967 to 1977.

On October 11th Mrs. Shirley Williams was the speaker at a 'United Act of Worship' to celebrate 'International Women's year'. In 1981 she was the first elected Social Democratic Party M.P. when she won the Crosby constituency by-election. There is a Halls of Residence at Edge Hill University named Williams in her honour.

On October 16th Lord Kenneth Clark (1903/1983), well known to television viewers for his series *Civilisation,* gave the address at a special act of worship designed to celebrate 'European Architectural Heritage Year'.

Mr. William Rathbone, who took on the editorship of the *Cathedral Bulletin* from Colonel Vere Cotton, retired. He was succeeded by Mr. Mark Holland.

The death occurred of Lord Cozen-Hardy (1907/1975), a director of Pilkingtons the glass manufacturers. He served as Chairman of the Stained Glass sub-committee and was a member of the General Committee from 1949.

The death occurred of Mr. George Pace (1915/1975), the Cathedral consultant architect, who specialised in ecclesiastical works in which he combined modernist and traditional styles.

A concert, by the German group 'Tangerine Dream' was held in the Cathedral.

After twelve years service Miss Hilary Leather, on her move to Cornwall, resigned from her position as Honorary Secretary of the 'Cathedral Friends and Builders'. She was succeeded by Miss Alison Tod.

Bishop Bickersteth of Warrington was translated to Bath and Wells where he served from 1975 to 1987. From 1979 to 1989 he also served as Clerk to the Closet advising the private secretary to the Queen on the names of candidates to fill vacancies in the roll of chaplains to the sovereign.

Mr. Ian Tracey (later Professor) was invited by the Dean and Chapter to be the Cathedral organ scholar for three years.

Mr. Alfred Turner (1879/1975), Honorary Treasurer of the Executive Committee from 1943 to 1967, died at the age of ninety six. His family presented two silver alms dishes to the Cathedral in his memory.

Mr. William Sheppard, the setter-out at the Cathedral site retired. He was succeeded by Mr. John Smart.

Carl Edwards (1914/1985), the designer of the West window, reported that his final piece of work in the Cathedral was completed. The window, which covers an area of 1600 square feet making it the largest window in the Cathedral, is named the *Benedicite* which is an ancient hymn found in the Apocrypha. Carl was trained by James Hogan and after service in the Second World War returned to work for Powells (Whitefriars) where he became chief designer in 1948. He left in 1952 to set up his own studio in Apothecaries Hall before later moving to the Glass House in Fulham.

## 1976

On January 27th The Revd Michael Henshall was consecrated Bishop of Warrington at York Minster by Archbishop Blanch of York. Before his appointment Bishop Henshall was vicar of St George, Altrincham serving from 1963 to 1976. Bishop Michael retired in 1996, the longest serving Bishop of Warrington. He was succeeded by the Rt Revd John Packer.

Mrs. Ethel Farnan, a Cathedral cleaner since the days of Dean Dwelly, retired in January on her eightieth birthday.

During Holy Week, Theatre Roundabout presented a play on the life of *St. Francis of Assisi,* to commemorate the 750th anniversary of the death of the saint. The figure of St. Francis is depicted in the *Spirit of Service, Te Deum* and *Benedicite* windows.

On May 12th a Thanksgiving Service was held to celebrate the centenary of the Mothers' Union. The Mothers' Union was founded by Mary Sumner in 1876 in the parish of Old Alresford near Winchester, where her husband the Revd George Sumner was Rector. In 2011 a Mother's Union was inaugurated at the Cathedral. The first Cathedral in the country to do so.

In May an 'Appeal' was launched to finance the completion of the building of the Cathedral.

On September 6th a Service was held at the inauguration of an exhibition of photographs tracing the history of Dr Barnardo's home for boys.

# 1976

*On December 1st Bishop David preached at a Service to celebrate the 10th anniversary of the founding of 'Shelter', the National Campaign for the homeless. The organisation did notable work in the vicinity of the Cathedral.*

A Fiftieth anniversary organ recital was held on October 23rd. A programme of recitals, arranged by Noel Rawsthorne, took place during the year to celebrate the anniversary.

In November The Lord Mayor of Liverpool, Alderman Raymond Craine sponsored an 'Appeal Meeting'. As part of the appeal to raise funds to complete the building of the Cathedral an exhibition with photographs of special events in the history of the Cathedral were displayed at the entrance to the Baptistery. The exhibition was staged by Mr. James Green.

On December 1st Bishop David preached at a Service to celebrate the 10th anniversary of the founding of 'Shelter', the National Campaign for the homeless. The organisation did notable work in the vicinity of the Cathedral.

A silver mace, designed and made by Francis Coote, in memory of George Alexander Nairn (1889/1974), was presented to the Cathedral by Mrs. Nairn and children. Mr. Nairn was a member of the Executive Committee and had succeeded Sir Alan Tod as President of the Cross Guild.

A wafer box, designed and made by Francis Coote, in memory of Emily Mabel Mather, was presented by a friend of Miss Mather. Emily Mather (1874/1976) was the daughter of Arthur. S. Mather (1843/1929), former Lord Mayor of Liverpool and a former member of the Cathedral Executive Committee.

An exhibition of stained glass by Carl Edwards, including his sketch for the East window in the Lady Chapel and the actual fanlight of the *Benedicite* window, was held in the Chapter House.

A Service was held to commemorate the 150th anniversary of the Masonic Province of West Lancashire.

The Most Revd Derek Worlock (1920/1996) on his appointment as the Archbishop of Liverpool visited the Cathedral to meet Dean Patey and Chapter. It was the beginning of a friendship with Bishop David, which witnessed their work for reconciliation. Together they produced the books, *Better Together* and *With Hope in our Hearts*. On Sunday May 11th 2008 during the Christian Walk of Witness the Sheppard/Worlock statue in Hope Street was unveiled.

Mr. N. Keith Scott was appointed consultant architect in succession to Mr. George Pace. Work began on building into the West wall the metal for the *Benedicite* window.

# 1977

Mr. Joe Ridyard (1897/1977), the Cathedral Tower Captain for fifteen years until his retirement in 1972, died on February 13th. Joe conducted the first peal on the Cathedral bells and for over fifty years he rang the bells at Christ Church, Southport.

On June 5, a Civic Service was held to celebrate the Silver Jubilee of Her Majesty Queen Elizabeth.

On June 19th a Service of Thanksgiving to celebrate the centenary of the founding of the St John Ambulance was held. The preacher was Lord Grey of Naunton the Bailiff of Egle, one of the highest offices in the Order. The St John Ambulance Association was founded in July 1877 to teach first aid in large railway centres and mining districts.

*The Sheppard/Worlock statue, design by Stephen Broadbent, was unveiled on Sunday May 11th 2008 in the presence of the Bishop of Liverpool the Rt Revd James Jones and the Archbishop of Liverpool the Most Revd Patrick Kelly.*

# 1977

*On June 21st, as part of the Silver Jubilee celebrations Her Majesty Queen Elizabeth accompanied by Prince Philip visited the Cathedral for the 'Festival of Youth' after first visiting the Metropolitan Cathedral.*

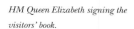
*HM Queen Elizabeth signing the visitors' book.*

On June 21st, as part of the Silver Jubilee celebrations Her Majesty Queen Elizabeth accompanied by Prince Philip, after first visiting the Metropolitan Cathedral, visited the Cathedral for the 'Festival of Youth'. The planning of the service, which included children from all over the city, was directed by Brigadier Sir Douglas Crawford who was Lord Lieutenant of Merseyside. He also planned the service to mark the completion of the Cathedral. To mark his Lieutenancy, Sir Douglas presented a ceremonial Mace. His name is recorded in the Presbytery.

On June 22nd the greater part of the Cathedral silver was stolen from the sacristy.

On June 23rd Sir Charles Groves conducted Mahler's *Eighth Symphony*. To celebrate the 50th anniversary of the founding of St Katherine's College of Education members of the College attended a Choral Eucharist on the evening of June 29th.

The death occurred of Bishop Clifford Martin (1895/1977). A Service of Thanksgiving for his life and work was held on September 30th. His memorial is to be found in the South Choir aisle.

As a result of a substantial bequest by Miss Mary Hoyle, of Cleveleys, Blackpool, the old embroidery room and vergers' vestry off the South East transept was converted into a central clergy vestry (now the staff room). The work was designed by the consultant architect George Pace.

On December 16th Brian Redhead's B.B.C. 1 programme *Home Ground* was devoted to the work of the Cathedral.

Archdeacon Eric Evans died on December 25th. The Cathedral organ was cleaned and the pipe work restored to its original condition. The work was carried out by Harrison and Harrison, organ builders, of Durham.

# 1978

*At 11am on Wednesday October 25th in the presence of Her Majesty Queen Elizabeth, the third and final Bay of the Nave was dedicated by Bishop Sheppard.*

Mr. David Wells took over the care and maintenance of the organ.

Mr. James Bainbridge resigned as managing director of Liverpool Cathedral Contractors Ltd. He was succeeded by Mr. John Smart.

## 1978

In January the Cathedral Committee's Bulletin was published for the final time.

The 'Commemoration of Victory in the Battle of the Atlantic' service took place on Sunday May 7th.

Bishop Sheppard invited a number of the Bishops attending the Lambeth Conference to visit the Diocese to engage in a 'Partners in Mission' exercise with the Diocese.

Churchwardens and church councillors attended 'Deanery Visitation Services' addressed by Bishop Sheppard.

A Commemorative Service was held on September 26th, the 150th anniversary of the birth of social reformer Josephine Butler (1808/1906). Her portrait appears in the Noble Women window in the Atrium of the Lady Chapel. In 1867 with her friend Anne Clough (1820/1892) she formed the North of England Council for promoting higher education for women. Anne's portrait also appears in the Noble Women window.

As final preparations were made for the dedication of the third Bay of the Nave it became apparent that the Great West Doors would not be completed in time. The limed English oak doors, each one weighing over one ton, were designed by the Cathedral architect Frederick G. Thomas. They were made and fitted in 1981 by Dart & Francis Ltd of Crediton, Devon. For their skill the company carpenters received the Carpenter's Award for 1981.

At 11am on Wednesday October 25th in the presence of Her Majesty Queen Elizabeth, the third and final Bay of the Nave was dedicated by Bishop Sheppard. The sermon, based on the text taken from Luke 19:39-40, was given by Archbishop Blanch of York and former Bishop of Liverpool. The climax of the service, which was compiled by Canon Naylor, was a choral work, entitled *A Song of Creation,* by John Madden a former chorister.

Archbishop Worlock from the Metropolitan Cathedral presented a Holy Bible to Dean Patey and the Chapter.

To commemorate the completion of the Cathedral the Appeal Fund commissioned a silver goblet containing a detailed engraving of the Cathedral and the Coat of Arms of the Dean and Chapter.

At the conclusion of the Dedication Service Her Majesty unveiled a stone, carved by Mr. Tom Murphy, in the South wall of the Nave Arch commemorating Her Presence at the service.

The Service of Thanksgiving marked the formal completion of the Cathedral which is dedicated to 'The Lord Christ in especial honour of the power of His Resurrection'. The Cathedral is the first 'mother church' to be built in the Northern Province of England since the Reformation.

*Liverpool will have a Gothic Cathedral, but of quite a different type to that of our medieval Cathedrals; in fact, there is no Gothic building in the world to which it can be compared.*

*Giles Gilbert Scott, 1904*

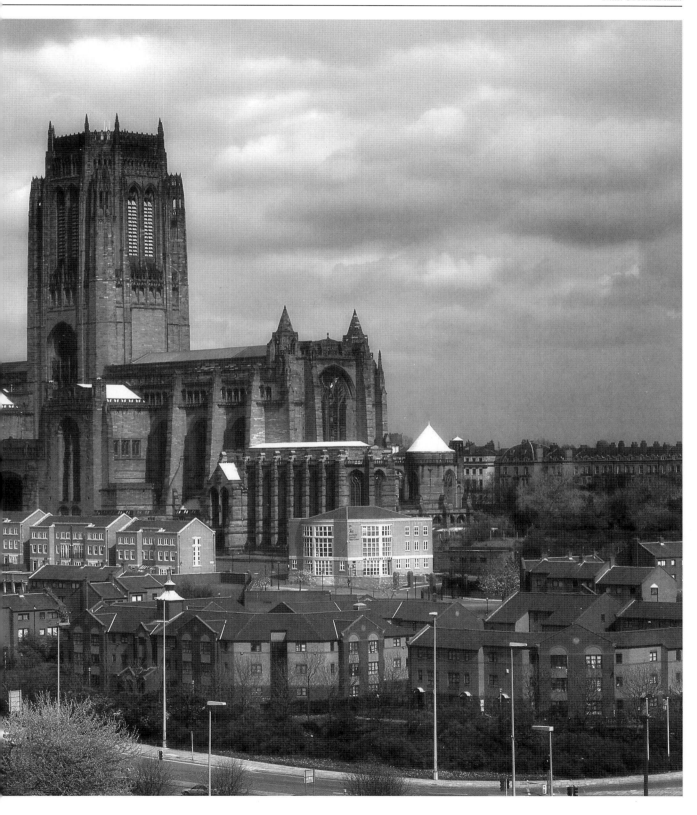

# BIBLIOGRAPHY

**MAIN SOURCES**

Liverpool Cathedral Committee's
Bulletin (1925/1978),
No's 1 to 100.

Liverpool Cathedral Newsletter
(1970/1979).

Liverpool Cathedral Builders
Bulletin (1930).

Liverpool Diocesan Centenary
Committee. Portrait of a Diocese,
1880-1980.

Liverpool Diocesan Calendar
(1916)

The Liverpool Review. Diocesan
Jubilee Number (1930)

Various Orders of Service

Friends of Liverpool Cathedral
Newsletter.

The Embroideries at Liverpool
Cathedral. Liverpool Cathedral
(2009)

The Stained Glass of Liverpool
Cathedral. A Pitkin Guide. (2002)

Newspapers

Liverpool Echo

Liverpool Daily Post

Cathedral Correspondence and
Photographs (Held in Cathedral
Archive Department)

Chavasse Correspondence
(Held at the London Metropolitan
University).

**OTHER WORKS**

Bassie G.F.
Liverpool's Finest. The history of
the city's Fire Brigade.(2008)

Beaken R. Cosmo Lang,
Archbishop in War and Crisis.
(2012)

Belcham J. (ed)
Popular Politics, Riot and Labour.
(1992)

Bickersteth J.
Run O'The Mill Bishop. (1992)

Chalmers W.S.
Max Horton and the Western
Approaches (1954)

Clayton A.
Chavasse Double VC (1992)

Coggan D.
Cuthbert Bardsley,
Bishop-Evangelist-Pastor. (1989).

Cotton V. E.
The Liverpool Cathedral Official
handbook. (1924)

Cotton V. E. The Book of Liverpool
Cathedral (1964)

Davies S. Liverpool Labour (1996)

Egan-Whittington. R.
Liverpool Roundabout (1976)

Forwood W. B.
Recollections of a Busy Life (1910)

Hemm Gordon.
Selected Drawings of Liverpool
Cathedral (undated).

Kennerley P.
The Building of Liverpool
Cathedral. (2008)

Lancelot J.B.
Francis James Chavasse,
Bishop of Liverpool. (1928)

Redman R. & Sands C. A.
History of Christ Church,
Bootle. (1979)

Redman R. & Sands C. A.
Bootle Milestones. (2006)

Riley J.
Today's Cathedral (1978)

Russell E. J.C.Ryle
That man of granite with the heart
of a child (2008)

Scott R.G.
Giles Gilbert Scott,
His Son's View. (2011)

Scouse Press.
Everyday History of Liverpool
and Merseyside (1996)

Sheppard D.
Steps Along Hope Street. (2002)

Williams D. Stuart Blanch
A Life. (2001)